and/or

word — image — provocation

Volume 1
Fall 2010

Editor-in-Chief
Damian Ward Hey

Art Editor
George Kayaian

Literary Editor
Tracy Kline

Managing Editor
Michael S. Russo

www.and-or.org

Cover Art, Rocco Capamezzo

and/or *is a journal for creative experimental writing and/or innovative graphic art. The journal seeks submissions from writers and/or other sorts of artists whose work openly challenges the boundaries (mimetic, aesthetic, symbolic, cultural, political, philosophical, economic, spiritual, etc.) of literary and/or artistic expression.*

For more information about this publication, or to submit work for consideration for future volumes, contact us at andandor@live.com.

CONTENTS

POETRY

AND/OR

Letter from the Editors

Welcome to the inaugural issue of *and/or*, a print journal devoted to experimental writing *and/or* art *and/or* anything in-between. Although we, the editors, had been thinking about beginning *and/or* for quite a while, we did not actually get down to business until August of this year. Once we did get down to business, however, the work was both easy and compelling. Things naturally fell into place once we had put together a web page stating our philosophy and calling for submissions. As founders of a fledgling publication, we are absolutely amazed at how much excellent experimental material we received from around the earth, from New York, to India, to New Zealand. Although the Internet has become a standard vessel for the dissemination of arts and writing in our culture, we are still awed by its amazing (and unimaginably fast) ability to bring together a wide, diverse community of creative people. Our first submission arrived via e-mail on August 17th, and by our October 1st deadline, the number of people submitting work had risen to well over 300—this for an unknown publication developed from scratch. We ended up choosing work from forty-four contributors, resulting in an acceptance rate of approximately 1:7. What this showed us was that there is a vibrant and engaging community of experimental artists out there. *and/or* will do its part, in this and in future volumes, to present the wonderful, provocative work of this community to the public.

Of course, the real challenge of the journal has been to decide which of the wide range of submitted work to accept. This challenge was made all the greater by the (dys)functional ambiguity of the word "experimental" in our statement of purpose. *and/or* received many submissions that were high quality but far fewer that were both high quality and experimental. What, after all, qualifies as good experimental art and literature? The question has been the subject of countless academic books and essays, and the answers, over the ages, have been myriad and contradictory. What is experimental to one person may be old hat to another. In general, we have sought to include works that represent as broad an experimental spectrum as possible. We have given preference to those works that provoke the reader or the viewer to question some aspect of tradition, convention, or expectation. We have looked for writing that teaches the reader how to read it, and art that teaches the viewer how to view it. And, in our evaluation of submitted work, we were not beyond the occasional outburst of: we know the good stuff when we see it!

Don't we all?

Now, whether we have succeeded in our goal of presenting excellent, provocative experimental art and/or literature to the public is not for us to say. Such must remain the purview of our readers. For our part, we will consider *and/or* a success if it contributes to our readers' appreciation of, and perhaps even yearning for, the experimental whenever and wherever it presents itself. Why? Because, simply put, we believe that experiment – trial and error, fooling around, taking things apart, putting things together, breaking and making rules, etc. – keeps art and literature a dynamic, evolving, and essential expression of human existence.

We hope you enjoy our inaugural volume.

Best,
Damian Ward Hey, Editor-in-Chief
Michael Russo, Managing Editor

October 31, 2010

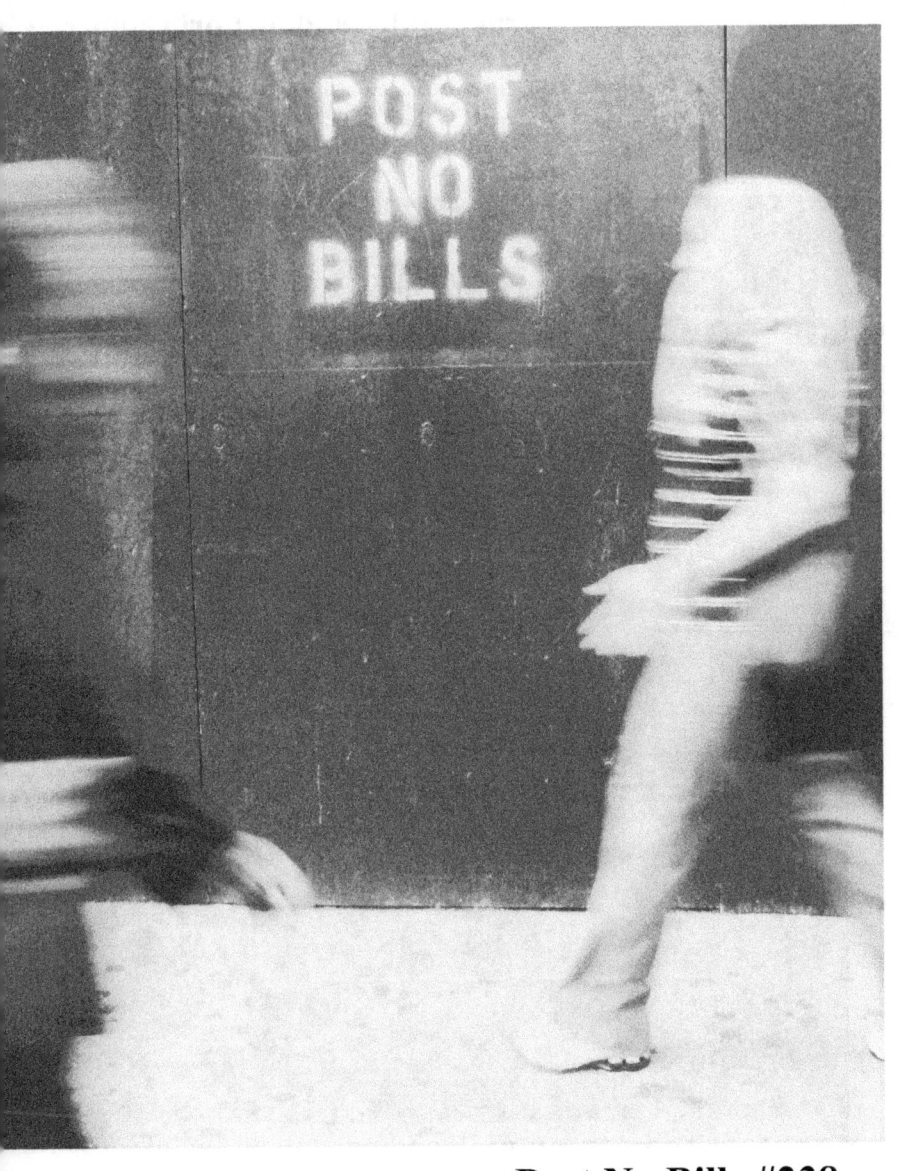

Post No Bills #238
Rocco Capamezzo

Poetry Publication Project Proposal
Bruce Stater and/or Lori Connerley

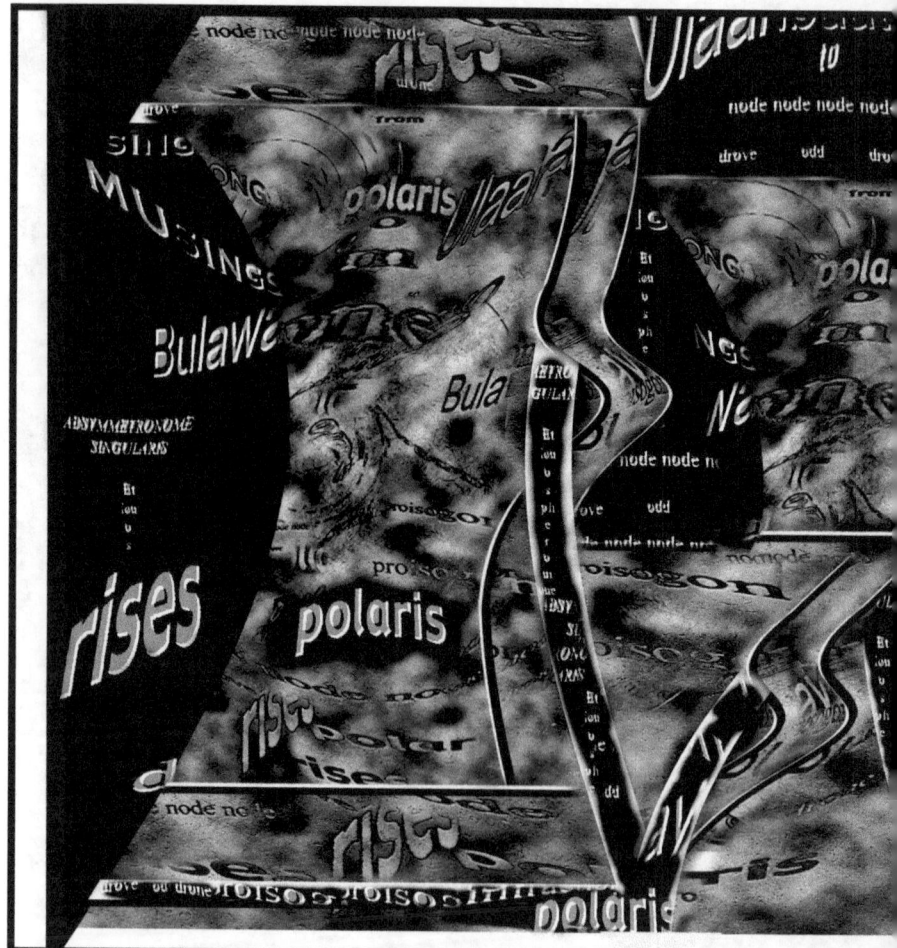

final singularis
Bruce Stater

Executive Summary

Objective

Either:

hamadryad telekinesis taraobolion particulate stratus colon angular parallel bars scoria ideogram terpsichore epigraphy seance period the number ten raised to the power one hundred dot cambrian oligocene mammalian diagonal line skeleton incantada tesseract epiphany slash whirlpool omniumgatherum realpolitik damselfly poltergeist logarithm aphasia yowl orangutan flotsam tautology heliotrope electromagnetism grapheme legerdemain ouroboros secret society ordinary language actions nostalgia grim empiricism low overhead headquarters in microscophilia slash provisional astrophysics reverse telemetry dash dandelion rhapsode orphism sea serpent dash routine experimentalism metaphysical archeology intuitive numerological database efficacious rhetoric diagonal line eschatology immersion transformative hierophanies erotic revolution or receptivity

Or:

historiography transforming the present situation period over period slash & slash. http://www/google.com/ the place where something was, is, or is to be located slash language games of the angels slash partial arbitrary refractive temporary dash destitute recalcitrant obscure sentimental sincere dash rainstorm emptiness monad artificial intelligence nomad dervish ecstatic regeneration slash astrictlylimitedchoiceordivisionbetweenonlytwooptions

And:

dot dot dot

Goals

Either:

having transforming transmogrifying permeating situating://
suggesting incorporating transcending evaluating serializing.

giving overwhelming organizing growing living encouraging.

caring occurring mesmerizing/

showing invoking telling emphasizing/

withholding ordering recalling demonstrating playing listening
announcing yowling offering flowering transcribing howling
empathizing glorifying losing opening signifying shouting
outraging laughing assembling negotiating gazing emptying
lighting opposing harvesting imparting making/

proposing articulating reversing thematizingdesiring

remaining overtaking segmenting singingremembering

evolving moving allowing involving demanding enveloping
                                                    retaining/
emoting inspiring taunting hoping establishing returning
                                    objecting revolutionizing

Or:
dash dash dash
dot dash dot

And:

dash dot dot

dash dash dash

dash

dash dot dot

dash dash dash

dash

dash dot dot

dash dash dash

dash

Solution

There is neither a determinate solution set nor a provisional one available at this time for this particular poetry publication proposal.

Creative Destruction (therapy)
Francis Raven

A case of mistaken identity
gets the whole psychology going

even though he's in both movies
and that guy who introduced me to so much art

said something like I bet Matt Damon just smiles
because he knows that it actually creates new emotion in the world

and I remember thinking
that he probably just wanted to fuck him

and this was just after I learned that
he picked up young boys

for his whole life
and it was a problem

something his lover called
a sexual addiction

and I remember thinking that I was really too young
to offer advice so I listened, but I did not become someone else

I wasn't really the type of person
who could become someone else

Besides, I wasn't really the type of person that melded easily into a
new fashion scene. Everything just sort of looked like me, which is
double-edged quality. But now I wanted it to be a perfect purchase:
to sum me up in this instant and to help me expand into my future
self.

But if it's possible
it says something about the actor;

if acting is possible
it says something about the actor.

———————

I remember thinking I'm not going to lose this book
and it's not like I lose a lot of books
but I remember thinking it in the New Orleans Airport
with Muffaletta smeared on my jacket
after your interviews

and then I lost it
by the plugs
that would not add juice

I like this point a lot.
"The former is made necessary by the latter"
is a very good way of putting it.

———————

It's a jacket that's brushed towards becoming

canned

as the heat causes the lid to seal

(the screwtop is strangely unnecessary)

even perishables such as yourself

can sit on a shelf

for untold months,   after which the piano

informs the audience of striving to be another

to let the bacteria infect the world

which is, of course, the cause of the current flu pandemic

(the umpire has called it, strangely enough)

which is, of course, the cause of such sentiments as

I think people need to stay in Mexico or in America and stop spread-
ing the flu by traveling

but strangely we keep moving around

trading and phoning and touching and gunning and drugging and
manufacturing and cooking and sleeping and marrying and selling
and eating and flying and driving and buying

but we're not the same, we're really not the same.

————————

Just as they meet in a foreign country under false pretenses…

they are allowed to be as different as You are allowed to be
as different
as

but when it comes right down to it

how different is the most different man from the least?

————————

14   *and/or*

They dive through binoculars
as you penetrate the distance between

the movie is a journey from true belief
to pure nihilism. Hence, the binoculars:

they will never find him. He will learn
not to panic. Growth will be awful.

But I lost the book and the moral of the book
had to do with making
not that poetry books
have morals
or main points
which I was never very good at ascertaining

the ailments that turn on the nose of a pin
that bleed

but we make with scraps what was intended for others. Hence,
I picture a frequent flier (for who is more probable?)
picking up the book
and at first dismissing it, then sort of cherishing it
but in a secret embarrassed way

like he probably wouldn't tell his wife
but he would tell himself that it caused him
to act differently

only no one could tell.

Finally, the impersonation reveals your true mission

which lists against the other's sails until you catch their eyes again via
your broken briefcase via your broken telephone: you have no
money.

This is a fact that they will overlook for so long.

_____

As singing together reveals your desire so hidden
and disgusting. The typewriter pleads for more money.
His glasses are the last to wake

just as wearing the other's jewelry reveals
the nauseating lengths
of gold chain
wrapped around your soul

or was that just your colon?
As the newly beloved launches out of the tub
heavy drips ruin the score on the emptying chessboard.

_____

As you first see the border of a father's letter
folded

> The poet folds meaning into meaning. Poetry is thus, a pro-
> liferation of folds of meaning, that is, of horizons of meaning.
> Philosophy is an attempt at unfolding the cloth in order to attain
> the pure presence of truth. (Expand!). (No).
> How are questions replied to, towards, poetically? Folded
> under themselves and therefore, almost unreadable. 'Reply' has
> nearly the same etymological structure as the verb 'replicate'.

To reply to something is to replicate that thing with a difference. Let us divide the act of replying into two entities: One, the thing which is replied to, which we will call, the ply, and two, the reply to the first ply. Is the ply an essence? No, it is a shifting bundle that is actually a previously enacted reply, but when it makes its appearance as the ply it necessarily appears as a fundamental essence. It is poetry that allows us to see that every ply is actually a reply.

Now it is time to play with the etymology of 'reply' and 'replicate' in order to let their poetries lead us. Both of those words etymologically mean 'to fold back' or 'to fold again'. So, a reply is a folding back to the source of the call and a replication is a folding again. If the replication is folded in exactly the same way as the original it is an exact replication. However, most attempts at replication are only approximate and thus are not exact replications but responses or replies. Poetry teaches us that every replication is inexact and that the source itself is just another reply.

Thus, what is a son supposed to do?

_____

We must make the replication ourselves
in the sleeping compartments' reflection
as it closes in on Rome and fate
and a new jacket: a blur of mountains
and responsibility. You know the lies are
piling, but the hypothetical job is accepted:

there is only one way to disprove an
IF X THEN Y
statement

if X occurs and Y doesn't

(X=True and Y=False) because if Y occurs
independently
you'll never know
if there was another antecedent
leading to our predicament. Thus,
we must make the fold ourselves.

––––––––––––––––––––

A new character mires our plans.
The booth is just for two.
You don't know anything about logic.
The tape is removed.
It is recording and removes the hair
painfully. Growth will be awful.
Eventually it will beat him to death
but before that
it will be merely awkward.

––––––––––––––––––––

They say the ticket is large parts.
A self larger than a man.
You look out on the ruins
and think someone made this
after which you are caught
in another man's clothes, don't say anything
please

the anxiety embarrasses to no end
but you simply must have breakfast

nourished, you think

––––––––––––––––––––

everyone who ever made anything was just a man

but not like me

is the thought
that runs through your head
as his girlfriend comforts you like a sister.

Isn't it pathetic? Don't you feel pathetic?

With the first dead body, the entire tone changes.

If everyone can make choices themselves
you have no obligations: isn't that convenient?

You know the arc from here.

As his obliviousness is at first charming;
As your taste merges for his benefit;
As the problem of the third is revealed to be you;
As your glance transforms into an ogle;
As the water opens to a new identity;

literally

the words cause the paddle to bludgeon
and create.

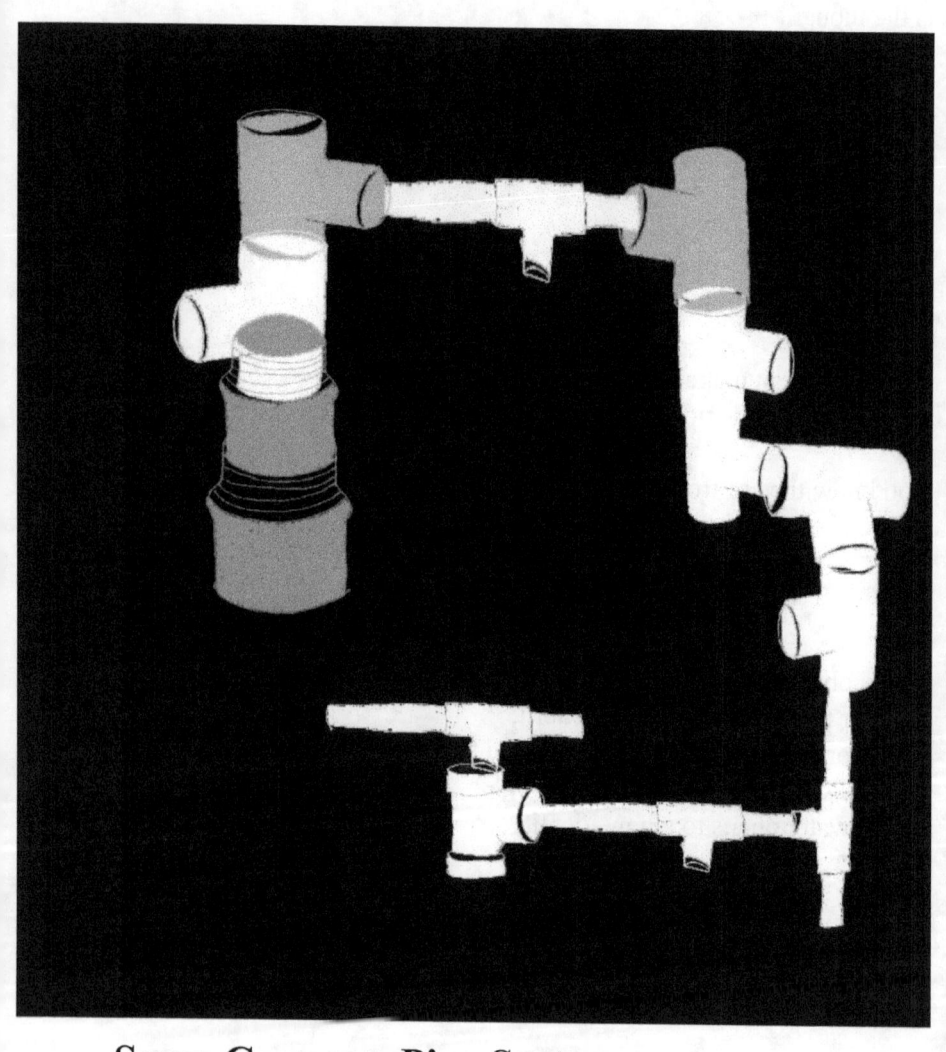

Some Common Pipe Systems
Francis Raven

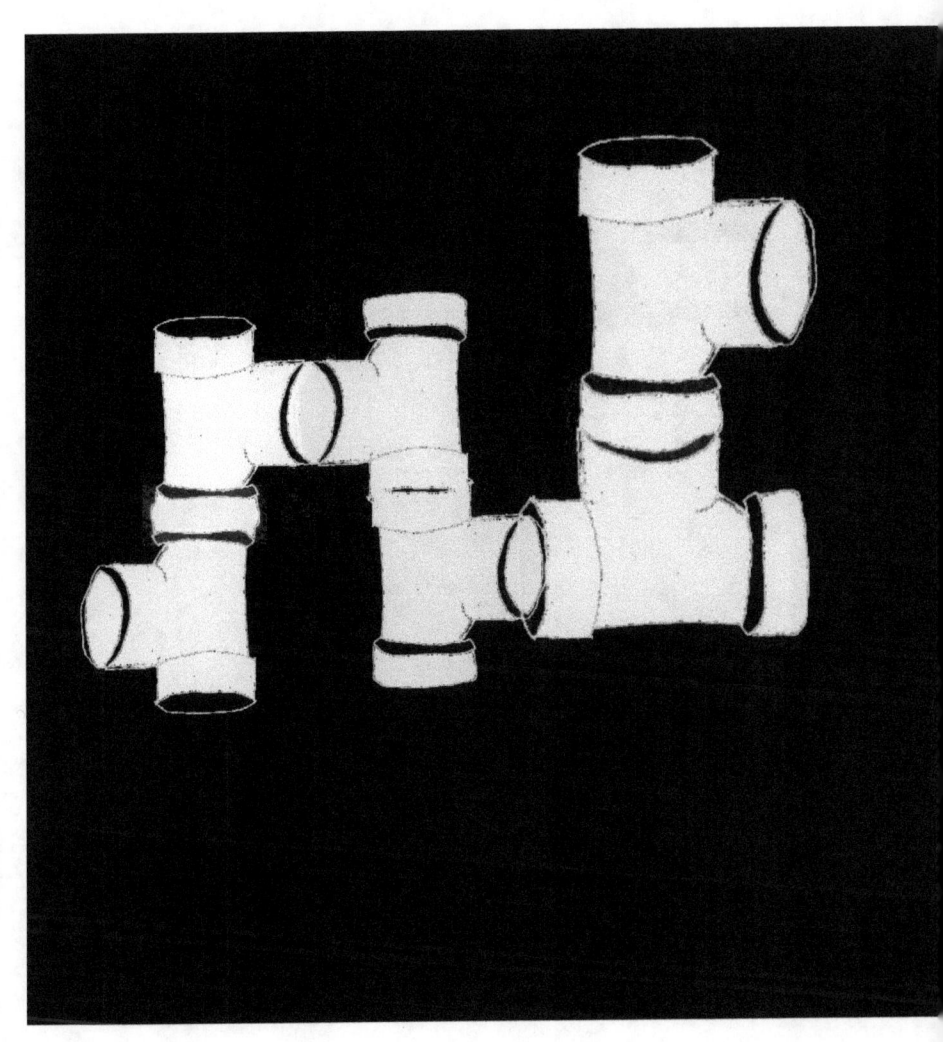

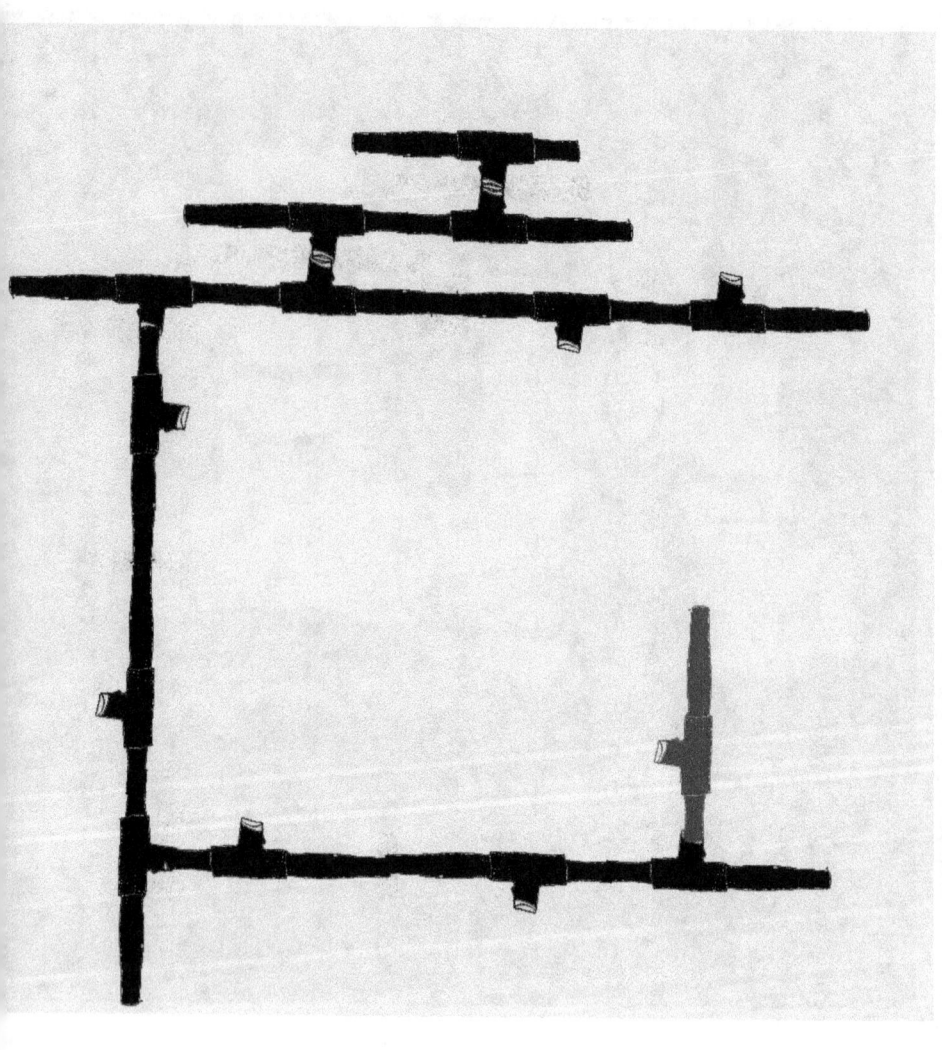

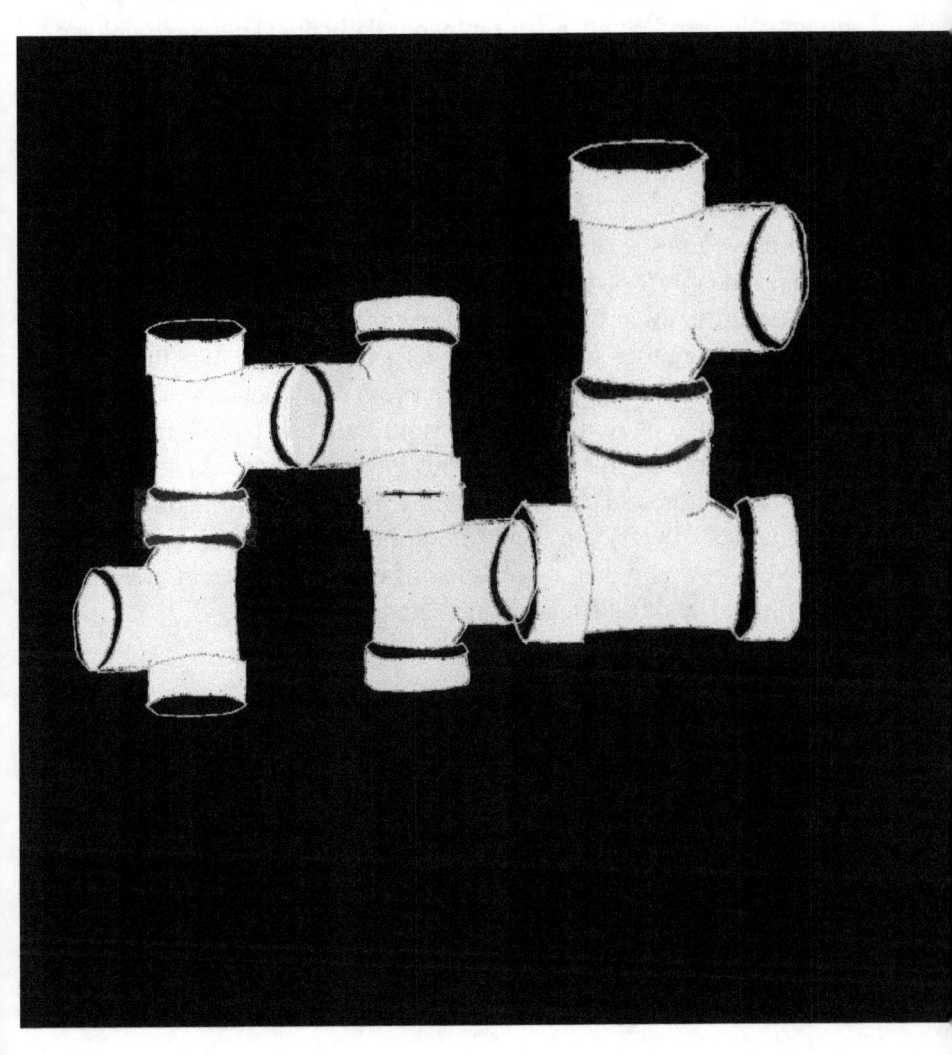

Ah Ha-Ha
Christina Murphy

Ah Ha-Ha. Something is stuck in my throat. Wonder bread. A white, doughy, lump of Wonder. Isn't it by our daily bread we earn our keep for the easy life or the hard? Ah Ha-Ha! Don't laugh—it isn't polite. Charm schools will teach you how to be polite and to dance the cha-cha-cha. Ah Ha! You know that Ha can be found in halo or hatred or hat. Or hand me my hat, please? The clock is ticking, the phone is ringing, it is time to la-la-la or Ha, Ha, Ha. What is your preference? What do you desire, long for, the most? Ha! So you won't say. Remember the giraffe we saw at the zoo? He didn't talk either, but oh what beautiful eyes! Please look at me with beautiful eyes. I need to feel loved more than you know. So let's dance—this time the tango. No! Let's do the hokey pokey. You put your right foot in. You put your right foot out. You remember your right foot, don't you? It's alongside your left foot—the one that leads the way, finds the path, avoids the road hazards, and carries you home. Home—ah yes, home. What about home? Hungry are you? I have the Wonder of Wonder Bread and every now and then a bowl-box of Cheerios. Cheerio, now! my sweet little Breakfast Blend. Run along home, Ha-Ha.

Guy with a Conductor Hat
Dawn Pendergast

It girl like a
mouse to
me, hulking, gutsome

verdict: sum swelling
scales hear me kiss big
the bellies
of my families below
triumphant
'heretofore'
-looking. \\

wear me tight pants
where going can tell
the future sex
of her mousewhite lob
iamb even
when off
(the lights are
when not, I don't)

mine balcony
configured
several tiers special
do i i do
out and nod
too made
like string
to her/hers
whitefleetensemble
flecked soup ice bob
in cold white
sunshone

sonnet on the back of a vintage mountain poem
Dawn Pendergast

will not / won't / walnuts
a because I feel orchard
the closetlight aglow in the heart of a tree
Give away it. will you.
Thethingis
Thethings is
things welt
things is long silt flections
harangue black pieces of
papernight
a zone one-notes upon a carpet
slipfaced
and I this amiss / morass
by sectional, by carpetlight

Man, Caged and Drawn
Mark L.O. Kempf

Discarded in the pub's hallway,
a piano – black, polished dust,
gouged ivory keys with blue lust
half peeled to the maple, thanks
to a flautist's punk-klezmer band.
Ghosts silently repeat the song-
4 minutes and 33 seconds,
all three movements, accompanied
by faeries, dancing as slow
as. This is
how we live with Mercy

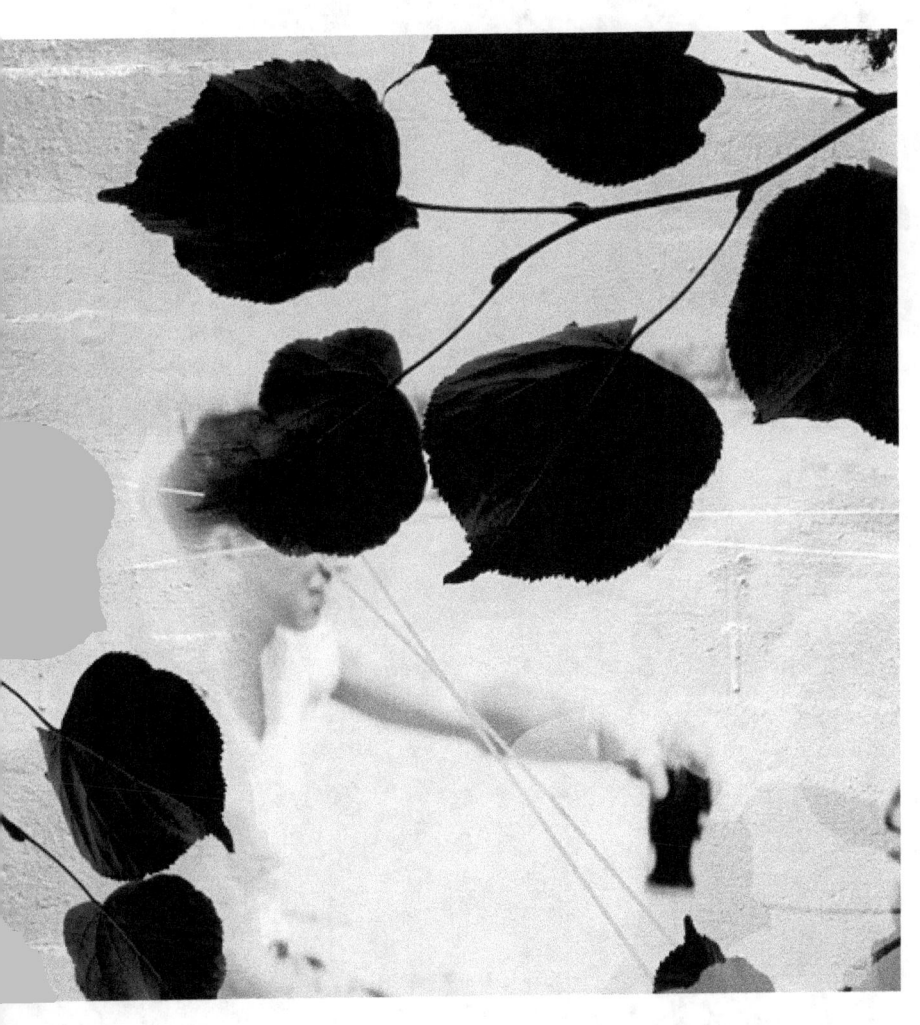

Self Imposed Aspergers
James Short

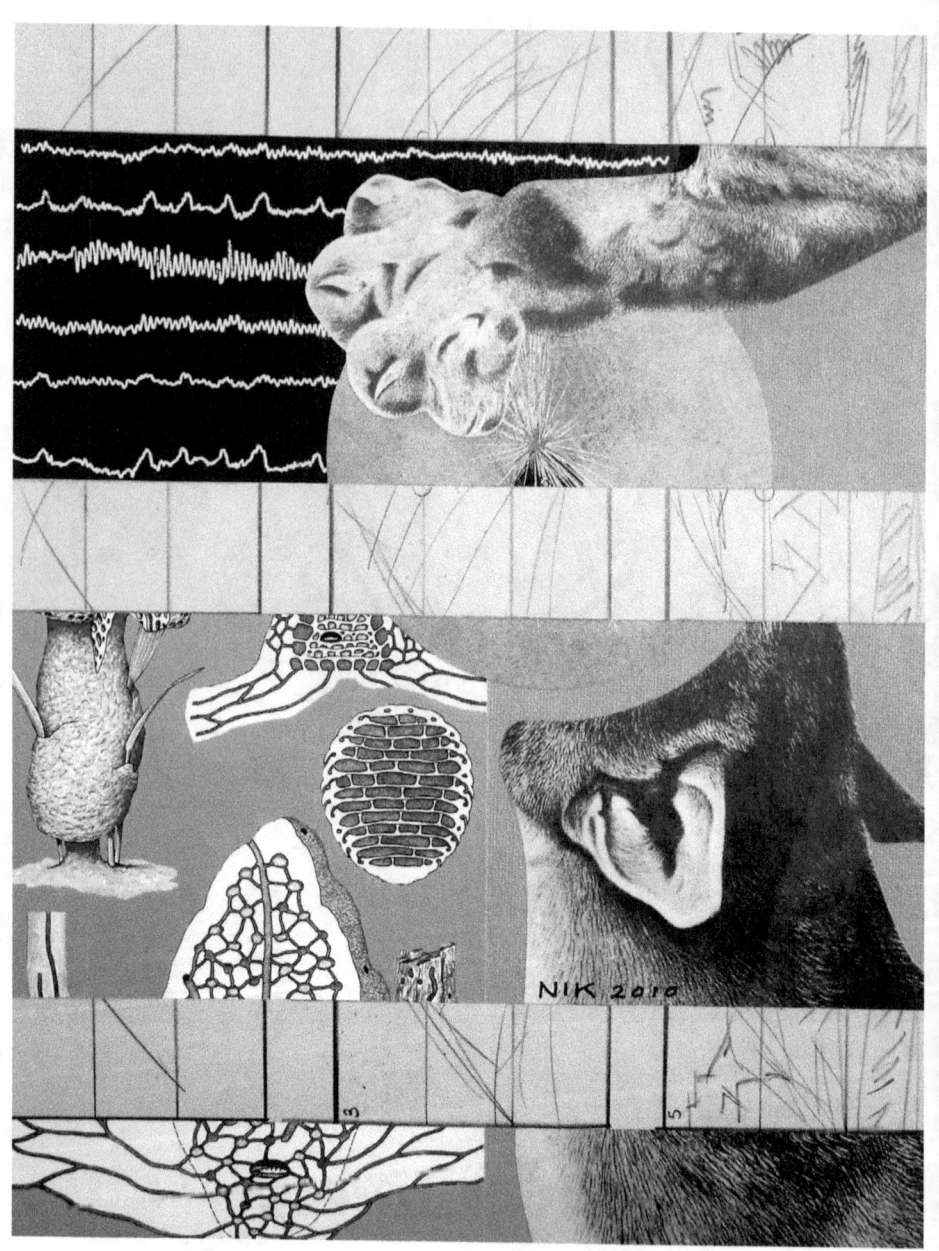

The Richness of Late Afternoon
Nicole Dahlke

I Got Yer "Grumpy" Right Here, Pal
Ron. Lavalette

I guess you'd be pretty grumpy, too
if you shared a crackerbox cottage
with six other chirpy little bastards,
up every day at the crack of dawn
with a merry Hi-Ho, Hi-Ho on their
lips, off to work after nothing but
a meager bowl of gruel, carrying
pickaxes and a box of dynamite,
leaving behind such a rare beauty,
a fair-skinned brown-eyed princess
to sweep up after them, make up
their beds, wash out their nasty
sheets, no one keeping her company
but a bunch of dopey bluebirds.
What a waste.
          And speaking of
dopey, let me just say a few words
about a couple of the schmucks
I work with:
          I busted a thumb
about a month ago and found out
Doc's not much of a real doc; and
I don't know what it is that keeps
that nitwit Sleepy nodding all day
or Happy so friggin happy, but
sooner or later there's bound to be
a cave-in and, frankly, I'll be glad
for the time off.
          Maybe then I'd
get to hang around the house,
see if the princess comes across
with a little TLC. Now, that might
improve my attitude some, eh?

Go away now, you're buggin me.

When He's Sixty-Four
Ron. Lavalette

He gets pulled over again, and this time
the cop is only about fifteen years old,
wants to know what's up; tells him
there's always been a stop sign at the
bottom of the hill; says he must be blind
or crazy, flying through there like that;
tells him he ought to turn off the radio,
get his mind on his driving.

                                He tells the cop
he's sorry; he says he was thinking about
his old friend John who got shot in front of
his hotel, right in front of his wife and
the cop says yeah well that's awful and all
but, still, ya gotta slow it down, Sir; gotta
slow it down and watch the signs or
you're gonna end up dead yourself
                —And he's not so deaf
he can't hear the condescending tone
in how the cop says sir; the way a bad father
speaks to a stubborn child—
                        The cop says
I'm gonna let it slide this time, Sir,
but, still, you gotta watch the signs.
                           Yeah,
yeah, yeah he says, I hear you. Signs.
Huh. Imagine.

Egg Test
Ron. Lavalette

This is Nish. Point
to Nish. Good.

This is Hondar.
Point to Hondar. Now
point to Nish. Good.

This is Kiptron. Point
to Kiptron. Good.
Now point to Nish.
Point to Hondar. Good.

This is uh, Whatsisname.
Point to whatsisname.
Now point to Hondar.
Kiptron. Nish.
Good.

This is a tough one. Point.
Good. Now Hondar.
Whatsisname. Nish.
Kiptron. Good.

Point. Point. Kiptron.
Good. Whatsisname.
Uh, point. Now Hondar.
Nish. Good.

Good. Good. Point.
Good.

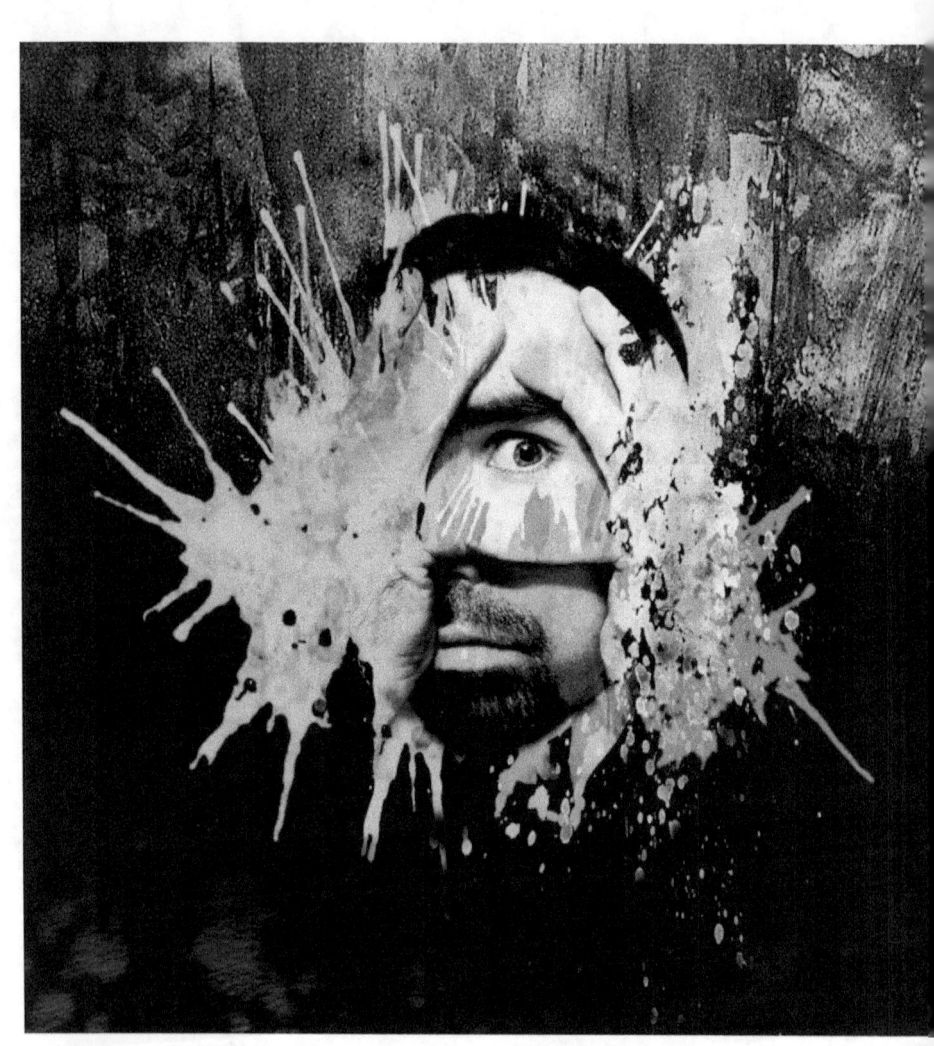

Swollen
Matt Parsons

Adam Fieled
from *Equations*

#36

Intermittence equations are relevant to every relationship. Most people love to have a lover leave and then return. The problem with Trish's return is that we still have the same problems we had the first time. We have burrowed too deeply into each other; Trish still enjoys sex in the abstract (as an element of Gothic fiction, with her as the heroine) more than she enjoys the physical act. As I get older, I want to give as well as receive pleasure; but Trish is never pleased. As my body satisfies itself, I realize Trish is not on the journey with me. Even a satiated body can get bored with its own satiety. We still escape into movies and marijuana; we still make an enjoyable spectacle as a couple. But too much needs fixing and fixing things is not usually a romantic process. We aren't effortlessly floating up from the surface; we're pushing through bullshit to find the surface again. Trish has no interest in fixing things; to be workmanlike is beneath her. So we hit the same old impasses and do the same old dances. When Trish flushes us this time, it sticks; when I feel uncharitable, I call her a female Peter Pan. Trish has turned intermittence into a stasis; she has frozen herself into her role as temptress, romantic heroine, Ophelia. Romantic heroines don't need to fix things; everything happens naturally, narratives move things along. But I'm in my thirties and I realize that when anyone hardens against changes, relationships become unworkable. Somewhere between Trish and Lisa, a happy medium exists— some reliability, some intermittence. As of 31, I haven't found it, and I become lost, up for anything.

#40

Oddly, Jena reacts against my middle-class roots, as if they are distasteful or deceitfully earned. Jena is demure and polite with my family; but there is an edge of defensiveness to her reactions. She shuts down rather than opening up, as Lisa does. When we sneak off to my bedroom to make love, Jena takes it as a welcome break and respite to duties and obligations she cannot, and will not, fulfill. She is proud of her family's nobility and simplicity; her ambitions involve maintenance of who she is, rather than a climb towards a new self, via material means. The truth, however, is that my family is far more friendly to Jena than her family is to me. Jena's family demonstrates no consonance with the arts; minimal conversational skills; insipid tastes; and the same edge of defensiveness that Jena has. So in-law miseries immediately begin to impinge on our little marriage. The only way Jena and I seem to work is alone; we thrive when marooned on little desert islands. We are so genuinely moved by each other's bodies that the relevant equation is simple: touch, touch, touch. I have more extended sex with Jena than I ever have with anyone else: hours after languorous hours, so that we are lifted up over our bodies simply from having emptied them. We're too young to realize how transcendental the engagement is— you could call it just kids being kids. But at least, not having delved into the normative crusts of ambition and betrayal, we do these things with the ripeness and purity that they can only have once.

#44

To be a young artist in the aughts in America— what could be a more daunting task? It's this Trish and I are escaping from; the sense that we are both fighting a tremendously uphill battle. We cower behind our years— we're young, in our mid-twenties, and we're not (necessarily) supposed to have scaled any mountains yet. We cower behind our dreams, our ideals; behind the inebriated joy of our bodies; and behind the consonance we have with dead masters. We train ourselves not to look at the odds, because the odds are against us. Yet we take for granted our own genius and the eventual dispersion of the world's riches at our feet. How seriously are we taken? We dismiss commentary from unenlightened sources which, if seriously considered, cuts off genius. How we separate is over discipline. My work ethic demands daily performance and permanent obeisance; Trish spaces things out so that many of her days are untouched by the rigors of creation. I drive hard at certain goals; Trish wavers between obeisance to her self-destructive impulses and her creative instincts. The net result of this contradiction is that she often has less to show for her efforts than I do. But we live in a time in which such distinctions are often unapparent; and I am more invested in Trish's eventual success than she is in mine. Her selfishness assumes too much— not just superior genius, but the laxity it can endow genius with. Assured of her future glory, she can intoxicate herself without due restraint. The darkness I sense in us manifests as an intuition that realities (especially political) are being ignored— that we are living irresponsible lives.

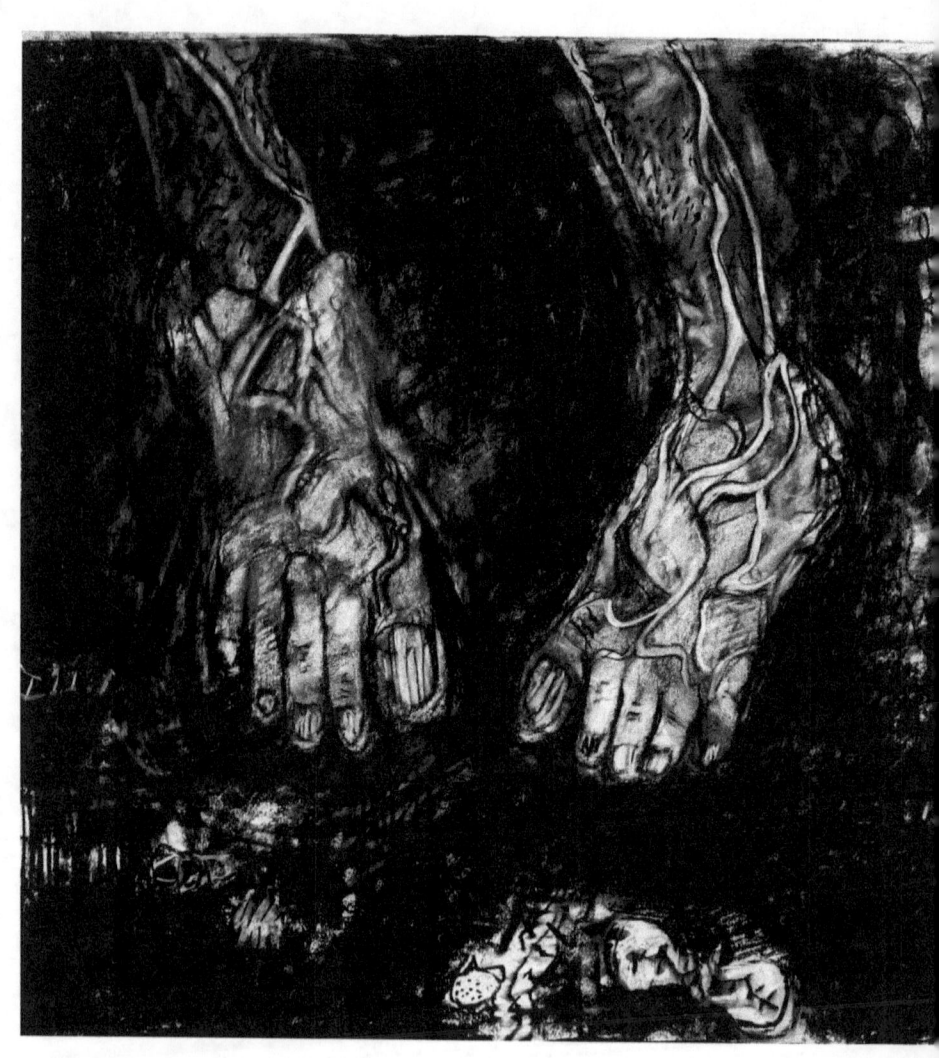

Darkest Ground
Justin Varner

Reader
Jenn Blair

My ears perk forward. Did that lecturer just say, "frighteningly democratic"? How startling. In America, we do not often marry those two words together. But I suppose the founding fathers knew there was such a thing. Attention: Second Eden starting up, Pronto. Help carve a new country out of (almost) uninhabited wilderness. Plenty of opportunities for advancement. On the lookout for: selfless, white, middle aged, English men with pale legs and powdered wigs, who can speak a smattering of French, read Locke and enjoy dabbling in amateur science projects (such as charting the Gulf Stream), in their spare time. All others need not apply.

Apparently, this type of exclusion can happen in literature as well. When people say their work is for "everyone," they might only mean everyone like themselves. People who live in trailer parks don't count. People who have never been to a big city to see The Phantom of the Opera or The Producers don't count. People who wear tube tops don't count. "Everyone" is everyone who donates their old clothes to Goodwill, and recycles their pop cans instead of decorating Naches Highway with them. We are talking about subtle people, the decent God fearers, meaning people who don't bring small shrieking babies to the movies. "Everyone" is "everyone proper." I am writing to you. But even as I tell you this, I'm secretly asking, "Are you like me?"

*

Sitting on the second floor of the library, I laugh at potatoes. In the 1700's, when they came for the first time in full force to the old world, many people were suspicious of them. One sect in Russia called them "apples of the devil" and thought for sure that potatoes were the fruit Eve ate in the garden. Another group thought that eating a potato would be like eating a soul. This was because all the potato eyes reminded them of a face. It is the funniest, saddest thing ever—that people were starving, yet scared of this strange new food, to the point that they refused it. I wonder if I ever ate my soul (or someone else's). If not, how else did it get inside me? Or is it inside me? If so, mine is more brown rough opaque skin, than eyes. I must not have eaten one with enough eyes. Next time, I'll remember.

I also read that hundreds of years ago, at a harvest festival in Eastern Europe, they believed it hurt the sheaves of wheat to be cut. I never thought that the grain might be galled to go down. But who really thinks that every bite they take is sacrifice? That it is death that lines our stomachs and plumps out our cheekbones. It is not such a pretty thought. It turns a mouth into a maw; it turns a swallow into a grave. It means I am staving off pangs by inflicting them. It means that when I cry, 'Praise the lamb,' there are chunks of bloody carcass stuck in my teeth. It means that unless mercy's in a good mood, I've got no home. Kathleen Norris' poem, On a New York City Bus, 1972, puts the predicament best: "The thing to do, finally, / Is to murder as little as possible."

*

Postmodernism. The windows of this house are mirrors. But keep looking out them. Go on drawing and detailing the countryside. We need to keep on keeping house. We might be underwater, but let's vacuum the carpet, anyway. If we are indeed underwater, we can match our surroundings, and have fish for dinner. Faces disappear, then re-merge as fragments. The cross is still worshipped, but only in splinters. One day you are Napoleon, the next, you are his great-great grandson, scooping up Neapolitan ice-cream, and wearing a hair net. You are on the coin. They won't let you toss it.

*

New Historicism—what kind of a tack is this? What is it called when you sneer at Pitt—an unlovely man with a name that is equally lugubrious—what happens when you fight fights, tip windmills over like sleeping cows, "dance a little dance"—parry, return a brilliant riposte—and all on paper—when you set out to tackle injustice by going to the fourth floor of the library and pouring over pulp? It's called spanking dead men's bottoms. It's exhilarating. But even as you are giving the swats, you look a little guiltily over your shoulder. A thought keeps coming back and grabbing your ankles. It is persistent and worried: Suppose there should be a reckoning? Once my dad came into my room late when I was supposed to be asleep. He found me hitting my doll because she was "bad." He told me if I didn't stop he'd have to take her away. I stopped. I didn't want him to take her. We decided she hadn't been THAT bad.

*

It is a lecture on Deconstruction and dear old Derrida. We are looking at his system, though it is not a system. We are trying to figure out how we can work with this theory, even if it is not a theory. We read a critic who asserts, "There is no limit to the number of selves an 'I' can have." These days I have been finding myself in the singular to be very tiring. In multiple? Too exhausting to think about (Rotting to their core on the shelves, are books grown so bored they are starting to read themselves).

*

Language is the problem. But, unfortunately, I can't get out of it and tell you all about it. I see what they are saying. I must speak to you, and you must speak to me, but the only way we can do it is words. We are in a monkey-house, a glass cage. We are so primitive, we even think in language. And a word has different connotations to me than a word to you. Above the bar appears a word we can all agree on. But underneath the bar, a fearful discrepancy might lurk. Say the word "Genius" to two middle-aged ladies. They both sit side by side very quietly, but one is picturing Stephen Hawking, and the other, Neil Diamond. I daresay, all we can have is a chat and some trouble.

*

Perhaps the only people who prattle on and on about the limits of language are the ones who never got picked first for baseball teams and read Robinson Crusoe five times. No one else is bothered. Housewives can use hammers and get a lot done. Only the carpenter stops, feeling something is out of place in his hand, fearing that he does not have the grip he (or she) ought to on the handle. But attacking language is the same as trying to beat a snake with one of those Egyptian Magician's staffs—no sooner do you grab the staff, than it turns to snake as well. It is advocating vegetarianism, but to be seen and heard, you have to stand on the platform of a pork chop. And then lug the smelly stage with you, from town to town.

*

Maybe there is a big balloon inside your head or your heart—a perfect buoyant sphere. But as it travels to your lips, it starts to shrivel up. When you finally open your mouth, all that falls out is a plastic shred—a piece of synthetic Kleenex gone through the dryer. Everyone stares. They, unimpressed. You, shocked and sorrowful. What a perilous passage! The widest chasm is not the space between the Inner and Outer Hebrides, but inward places and their outward expression. The balloon deflates so fast, and yet, you still hold out hope for next time. That next time a little less air would be lost before this world-on-a-string hits the world of the senses and gets shocked, just like blood does when it suddenly turns red, indignant at oxygen.

*

They give us the road report. Right outside Glasgow, the traffic is "head to tail." This seems better than "bumper to bumper" when you remember that some of the ancients drew a serpent biting its own tail to symbolize eternity. If you are sitting in your car with black ice outside and the radio is playing nothing but advertisements, forever is not blissful harps dripping off trees. If you cannot see time's head or tail, you might consider grabbing up your own tail and starting to munch—just to get some action.

*

When things happen across the sea, this is how they report it: Stateside, Blah-Blah occurred…Stateside makes me feel as if my country was a ship. I don't know port from starboard from stateside, but I guess it is still out there floating. Stateside today, a woman eating at a restaurant chain got a fried chicken head in her fried chicken. She was talking to her daughter and almost didn't notice it. It was a whole head, and a beak and feathers were still accompanying it. Whichever side Stateside is on, I need to know. I am thinking about heading on over to the other side. To throw up.

40   *and/or*

*

I hear that tomorrow we can expect "a band of cloud" coming in and snow on the mountains. A "band of cloud" sounds exciting. Just like the Sherlock Holmes' story titled "The Speckled Band." The "speckled band" turned out to be nothing more than a plain old snake, but the allure was in the phrase and the fact that I did not know what it meant. As long as it was the "speckled band," it wasn't just a coily, oily tongue darter—it was mystery itself. And tomorrow, it shall be hanging in the sky.

*

"Treading the boards," is what they call it here, meaning acting. I remember hearing a director ask once, "Why do they come—on either side of the lights? What is that about?" I am not sure I could tell her, except that maybe we are like moths. Drawn. To tell stories and be told them. Treading the boards reminds me of treading water. You just want to see how long you can do it before you sink. Treading is kneading, beating your knuckles in dough—you tread boards, knead bread—you can't walk on water so you walk on wood—you throw some floor, some flour around, and hope the end of the mess is sustenance…for someone.

*

In the train station at Edinburgh today, the computerized message board on the wall of the station announced that some trains would be delayed because of a "land slip" somewhere around Durham. "Land slip" sounds so much more polite than "land slide"—it's not a split and a whoosh, it's more like giving away something that should have been kept under wraps at a cocktail party. Oh my, I forgot…I don't think they are announcing to everyone that they are expecting quite yet. Oh, it's all right, Luv. Don't worry. The secret is safe with me. "Land slip" is just an inch or two of indiscretion hanging below respectability's hemline.

Last week, someone wrote into the paper, asking why it was the custom here to say, "Charlie's dead," to a woman when her slip was showing. The columnist replied that when Charles was killed in the seventeenth century, and Cromwell and the Puritans came to reign, the Roundheads' somber black clothes made sharp contrast to the frills and lace of the court and Cavaliers. So, anyone who had a bit of errant finery peeping out got reminded that Charlie was dead. And the tradition stuck.

A friend in Pennsylvania heard it like this from some women at her church when she was seven: "Dear, it's snowing down south." "No, it's not," she cheerily chirped back, "I talked to my grandparents down in Georgia yesterday and they said it was warm." Since their sweet politism undaunted her, they were forced to just tell her the truth. Her slip. When is it that we stop expecting people to say what they mean? It seems an odd fracture, but if we never make the break, society looks quite impossible.

*

What is the ego? And where does it live? I didn't know when I was a kid. A children's book I got from the library first introduced me to the mysterious word. In the story, the girl's father played tennis and had gotten scraped up on the court. As he lay on the couch, the girl asked him if anything had been seriously damaged. "Just my ego," he told her. From my acute acumen and literary skills, I pieced together that the ego must either be on the forehead or somewhere around the knees (the two places where the book mentioned he had icepacks). Since then, I have learned the ego is not around a mysterious bend in one's anatomy, but inside, hidden, and thus, even more dangerous. It simmers on a back burner of brain. Usually on low, but occasionally, the most fearsome flames will leap out.

*

She is a professor, with a smile as sweet as your grandma's, but a mind lithe as Blake's tyger with gleaming eyes. When we are going over psychology and the development of language, she keeps bringing up her firstborn son who is a toddler. She tells us he used to howl a fit when she left him at the nursery. He stopped, tho, soon after he learned the word, "goodbye." When he said the word "goodbye" out loud, he was in control of the situation, and his brain registered that she would be back. She has also noticed that when he feels threatened, he responds by tugging on his ear. I don't mean to be unfeeling, but it does not seem like she has a child so much as a little science experiment. I think I prefer my mode of upbringing. My mom put a shirt on me that said "handmade by God," and left me and my sticky graham cracker mouth and frizzy hair and tiny potbelly at that. Assuredly the best method for an article such as me.

*

A friend tells me her history professor is that man I always see in the library—the one who wears an olive green army jacket and a kilt, and is bald. She says he is from the Highlands, and has second sight. And he doesn't like to talk about it much, the things he sees, but once he did see his mother dead. And she wasn't even dead yet. What a thing it would be! To see the dead living and the living dead. But he always looks so quiet and composed, sitting down here in special collections reading. Perhaps this room with the glass window is safe. So I won't worry, but go back to looking at Joseph Brand's Antiquities. Brand is discussing those small white specks that sometimes appear in people's fingernails. The "vulgar" (or whoever those old ancestors of ours were), thought the number of them you had portended how many gifts were coming your way.

These white specks might also be consolation prices for those of us who have no second sight—if you cannot read the heavens, then turn your nails into ten tiny screens and watch what ships might be coming up on the horizon. Those were the days when old men dreamed dreams and the young men, visions. Then and now, all the rest of us can go get manicures.

*

As I try to sit here and study, one dream keeps re-occurring. Or is it a picture? One I've had for years now. It's not much really. A stainless steel sink below a kitchen window. In the sink there sits a bowl full of water with red-red apples floating in it. It is Autumn and outside the window, a road, a field. There is late afternoon sun turning the landscape's intensity up—light is streaming through, charging the apples till they glow and now you are not sure, not sure at all if they are red or gold. That's what I wish for. To me it seems absolutely everything one would need—stillness and promise, vague sadness and yearn-ing—Irving's Ichabod about to stroll by on his way to visit Katrina. A silver drop of water wriggles out of the faucet, dropping down like a diving fish. I stand there steady, a woman in a window—watching the richness of decay. I am the center of the universe in a side room, my plainness and quiet the lynchpin that bolts one hemisphere to another. I am the one who is keeping the heavens slack enough to roam in yet taut enough to tread on. I don't achieve the feat by baking bread. Or even being kind. I hold it all together, just by standing there. Like I said, it's nothing really. Some fruit. A window. A sink.

*

Why don't they tell you! Not to fall in love with all this—the arch of a stone bridge, arch of foot, of fish, of mind arcing its gleaming body out of the water for one glorious second before it gasps, falls back. Why don't they tell you history is not the dead buried over there, not lines on fields? History is the dead busy inside you, pulling you down, lifting you up, cheering you on, leaving lines in your palms—so you pick up your pen and busy yourself with lines on paper—letters you will never send.

Instead, we are dressed in pink, blue, given a watch eventually.

And still, the bulk of the inheritance is always bequeathed in the si-lence—and my ears are as fine as anyone's, I think. And mother loves me. And father thinks I'm quite smart. It ought to be enough to staunch this flow, this foolish flow of blood running out to the sandy waste, this tide that still goes out on the hour and returns to me no one. To-night I found out Virginia Woolf drowned herself. And am upset. Can't the dead, if anyone, be decent? Refrain from doing such disagreeable things?

*

I am a Protestant. Anne Sexton said of us, "Those are the people that sing/When they aren't quite/sure." And I'm not even quite sure I can sing. Snap-Snap. If anything is holding, holding a note, it's not me.

*

A professor says the anecdote can tell us so much about someone. For instance, William Hazlitt loved a girl. Madly. He even left his wife to be with her. But when he came back and told this girl he'd gotten a divorce, she was aloof. He flew into such a rage that he picked up and smashed to smithereens the statue of Napoleon he'd given her—and he loved Napoleon. It's just a moment of sheer feeling—and it speaks more than a thousand strands of dry pontificating and explication woven together. Yes, but what anecdote should be yours? Or mine? Will you remember something really kind and noble I did—something selfless? (Oh, but if it truly was selfless, I suppose you did not see it). How about you remember the night I had a new shirt on and my pants weren't wrinkled and I was in such fine form I could have beat Socrates at Scrabble? But you won't. You will seize on that time I was in such a frantic hurry to use the restroom, I dropped the back of my overalls into the toilet.

*

Dorothy, Dorothy. She had a chair labeled "G.K.C." after Chesterton, a writer she respected—but she did not simply name the chair out of reverence: the chair's wide girth invited a comparison. And that is the thing about Ms. Sayers. She is not nice when you'd like her to be. One gets the sense that she shouldn't stand out in your mind like a silhouette, but is rather, something solid to be run up against. She drank and smoke and talked about her soul every day, thank you very much, but not with the people who were narrow and so apt to look shocked, hurt, worried.

She is not cooingly maternal about her son. Not even maternal, really. She never told anyone but her cousin Ivy about him. The man she really wanted, John Cournos, left her because she would not live with him outside of marriage and use birth control. Eventually she did have a child. The father was a lump of a guy who lived above her and took her out on motorcycle rides. He was not, she told her parents, "literary" smart, but he knew about fixing boats. He visited her family's house once, but her parents never knew anything else about him or the baby. It's such stern pride. And yet, there is nothing of the sort when she writes to John Cournos and tells him of her child. She will meet Cournos if he'd like. They can still talk, just not of generalities—"Good God!" does he think she is "unsexed"?!! "Judah, with all thy faults, I love thee still," she told him. It's too frank to be passionate. You would think it'd be just what a man would want: someone who could manage to talk of the most emotionally taxing things in business like terms. But maybe it was too much of what a man wants—and when it comes right down to it, some would rather live with less. How it must have hurt, like hammer on thumb times ten, to hear that Cournos did eventually get married—and to a woman with children! Later, she got married too. Her mother asked what she wore. Green. She wore green. There are lifetimes and worlds swirling in that color, a forest of things revealed in that word.

*

If you think you can trust books, well, ha. We must be aware of the book as a thing. We must know that the editor is a human, and has his own crafty editor agendas. Look at this, the grad student tells us, as he hands out a photo-copy of a passage of Shakespeare. Here, Pope has put that Antony and Cleopatra hug, but Shakespeare never had them hug! And that hug, that press of the flesh, can change the whole scene, especially for the audience who knows nothing of the original author's intentions. The grad student tells us that when some student was handed Shakespeare as the playwright would have been read in his own day, the student gasped. "Good God, it looks like Chaucer!" he exclaimed. I am surprised, but I shouldn't be. I should remember that we are always making things change with us, even as we stay the same. I already knew that we couldn't trust the Greeks when they came bearing gifts. Now I know that we can't trust editors either. I still read the nutrition labels on my cereal box as creed, but oh, trembling, trembling. But of course, I already knew that. I already knew that when flesh presses, everything changes.

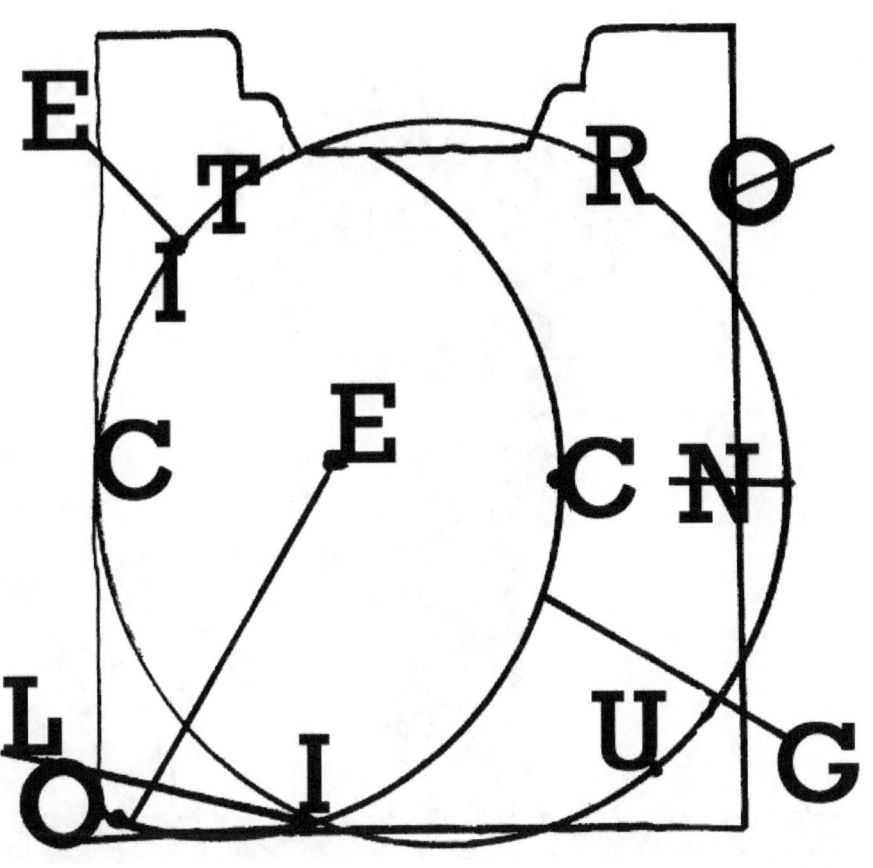

4&5
Tray Drumhann

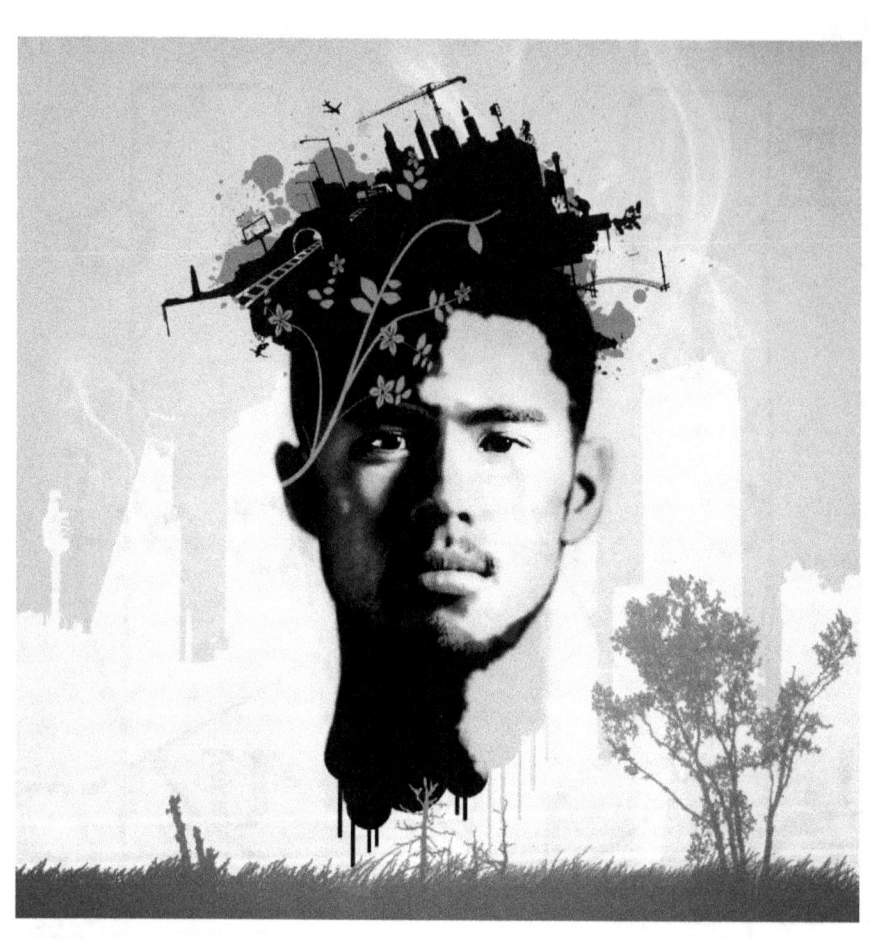

City Delirious
Matt Parsons

Woman Sleeping
Carolyn Agee

Her wizened skin covered by a single cloth,
soaked in waste seeping through the door.
Her exposed ribs move slightly in rest,
despite the rattle of the train.

I step over her, to the lavatory
where the walls are stained with blood, faeces—
the scent of rotting palms.
I stagger to the hole where I piss
on the tracks to hell.

Physical for an Old Woman Picked Up Wandering
Donal Mahoney

Between her legs
the doctor found a goatee

gray as city pigeons
flying through factory smoke

a goatee that hadn't been combed
that hadn't been kept

that quit in fangs
an inch above her knees

John Gotti O.G.
Brian Cogan

Despite our closeness, I believe that I learned of the death of John Gotti just as everyone else did, via secret messages left in a hidden drop spot behind the third toilet to the left in Grand Central Terminal. As I unwrapped the layers of newspapers, my hands shook in anticipation. I knew that John was sick, but he had always told me in that gruff but lovable voice of his, "Throat Cancer, throat schmancer! It's just a little agita." Then he would slap me on the back, and I would slap him back, and he would glare at me and darkly mutter, "Don't touch me." Then we would both laugh and laugh. These happy memories could not overshadow the hollow feeling I felt as I unwrapped the last layer of "The Bergen Record" to see the grim visage of a dead chipmunk wrapped in walnuts with just a hint of fennel. A Sicilian message that the "Dapper Don" was indeed gone.

As I grieved for the loss of a dear friend, I remembered the first time I had met Gotti. I was a young hip-hop promoter in the Bronx and was organizing the last of several DJ battles that would determine which DJ would be considered the most "def" and would earn the right to wear the coveted "def Forever" t-shirt for the rest of that week. Competition was based on scratching, ability to manipulate break-beats, creative use of sampling, and the ability to recite epic sagas in their original dialect. Usually Kool Herc or Afrika Bambatta would outstrip the competition through their experimentations with polyrhythm and iambic pentameter, but this time a cocky young kid from queens won by matching the drum break from James Brown's "funky drummer" to a marathon recitation of the "Song of Roland." I knew I had to meet this young turk, and after a few minutes of being manhandled by several members of his "posse"(including DJ Cool Sal the Butcher and Terminator "the horse" X), I was introduced to the great man, himself. I congratulated him on his victory and, as he draped the prize shirt over his massive frame, he muttered to me, "S'nothing dawg, just trying to keep it real, aight?" We became quick friends and, for the next several years, he would call me late at night to discus the relative merits of some new house or techno 12" or warn me ominously about "sucker mc's who refused to call him sire" who were going to be taken care of at some point in the future. I told him to try and relax, but by that point I think that the weight of his new position, head of the Fraternal Young Man's Association of Law-Abiding Italians, was beginning to give him some stress, and while his growing influence within the hip-hop and dance communities was unassailable, even as a fan, I had to admit that his last few 12" remix's were derivative of Detroit House.

Then came John's persecution. As usual, it was by the man. Apparently, he had been sonically and criminally a few years ahead of his time, and this did not go over well with haters and law enforcement alike. At the same time, I could feel a growing gulf between myself and the man I would have trusted with my stylus. By the late eighties and early nineties, we had begun to move in different directions -- me towards a new sound, more influenced by classic euro-disco and Brit-pop, and him towards more of both a rap-rock fusion and control of gambling and the construction industry. Even though his legal difficulties kept him busy, I would see him at night, sometimes at Sound Factory in the old days, and sometimes after-hours at Twilo. Even after his celebrated "trial" and "betrayal" by Sammy "the" Bull Gravano, he was secretly still allowed by the authorities to attend to many of his party promotion gigs, even while serving hard time. When I asked John about how prison was treating him and if he was still "keeping it real," he would just laugh and mutter, "s'aight," and then he would slap me on the cheek, and I would slap him on the cheek, and one of his goons would break my left kneecap. I knew that he did this out of love, and I asked two of his closest associates, Tony The Lemur and Suge Knight, if Gotti really respected me or simply thought I was "old school," but they just smiled and broke my right kneecap. Then we all laughed and laughed.

As his health began to fail, I began to see less of him on the club circuit. I'm not sure if it was the massive "peace-pax" rave at Ibiza, or the "pax-peace" rave in Tel Aviv in 1999 where I saw him in person for the last time. He looked tired, and we didn't get a chance to talk, but as I mixed "Apache" by Michael Viner's Incredible Bongo Band into Bobby Digital's "Glock Goes Pop," I could see him acknowledge me with a wry grin from across the crowded dance floor. A few moments later, a package arrived at the DJ booth containing a bottle of anisette, a cured Genoa sausage, and the preserved remains of an Etruscan ax handle. The combination of food, drink, and archeology was an ancient Neapolitan sign of respect, and I felt at that moment as if I had finally arrived. I saluted him with the traditional "west side" symbol of gangsters everywhere, and he weakly, but respectfully, waved a glow-stick back in my direction.

And now that John is gone, I think it is too late to evaluate his influence on numbers running and too early to analyze his influence on two-step and jungle. No matter how history will judge the brutal beatings and contract murders, I think that even his main detractors will agree that, as long as people are willing to break it down funky on the dance floor, the name John Gotti will never be forgotten.

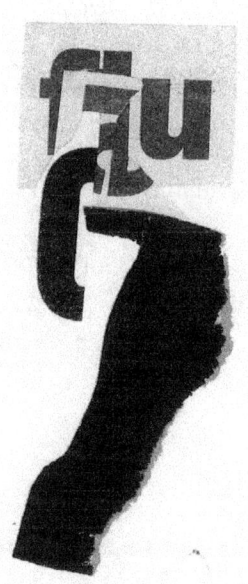

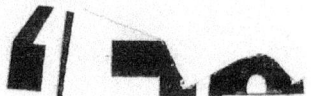

Flu
RC Miller

after brain trauma
Orchid Tierney

I Love Lucy   Proxima Centuri
canned applause   wavelengths
broadcasting

        distending

           clowning   Hollywood
    three hundred thousand   Tropicana
      kilometers   Ricky   per second
electromagnetic   heart on satin

         frequencies
         attenuating

until   only
stars   will hear us   laugh

engineering butterflies
Orchid Tierney

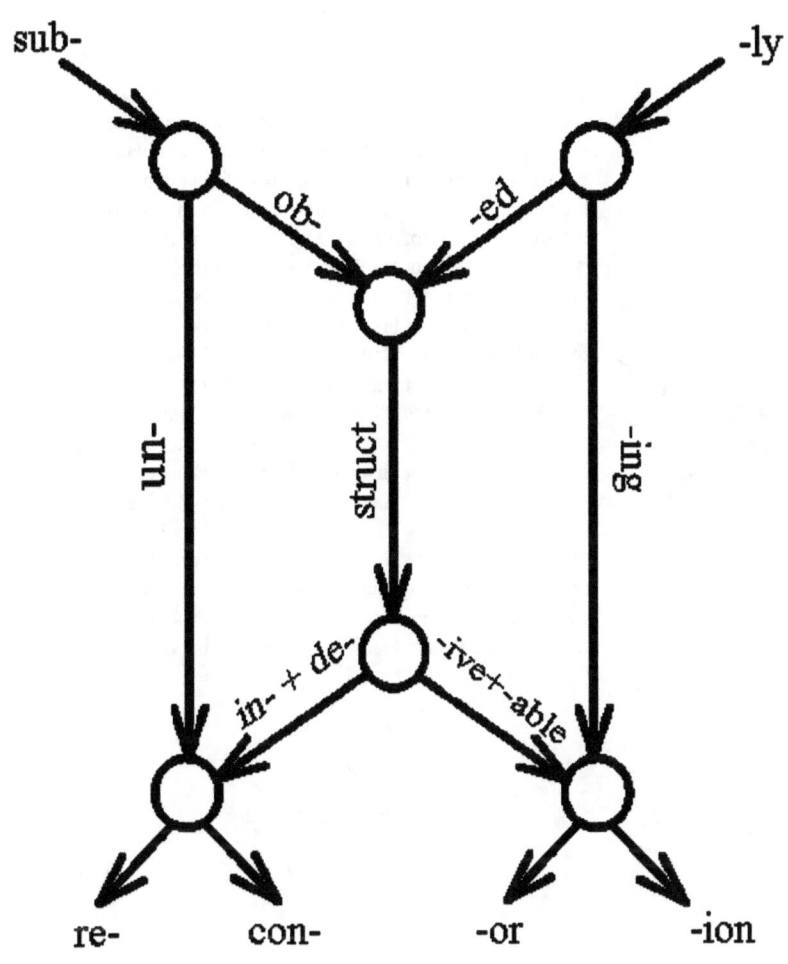

Reading Critical Theory
Orchid Tierney

the white page is not blank the white page is not blank
the white page is not blank the white page is not blank
the white page is not blank the white page is not blank
the white page is not blank the white page is not blank
the white page is not blank the white page is not blank
the white page is not blank the white page is not blank
the white page is not blank the white page is not blank
the white page is not blank the white page is not blank
the white page is not blank the white page is not blank
the white page is not blank the white page is not blank
the ~~author~~ does not exist the ~~author~~ does not exist
the white page is not blank the white page is not blank
the white page is not blank the white page is not blank
the white page is not blank the white page is not blank
the white page is not blank the white page is not blank
the white page is not blank the white page is not blank
the white page is not blank the white page is not blank
the white page is not blank the white page is not blank
the white page is not blank the white page is not blank

scriptor
reader

signs
radar

myth

[fig. 1] reading critical theory

Reading Critical Theory
Orchid Tierney

Language is a broken system. Meaning is a virus where signs become fragments, symptoms

like photographic stills of space.

However, space and time are internal mechanisms within our individual, human universes

clause conjunction clause comma clause (stop) clause semicolon clause comma clause stop
clause comma clause (stop) clause bracket *latin* bracket clause comma clause comma
dependent clause coordinator clause colon noun conjunction noun stop clause comma
clause coordinator clause comma clause comma dependant clause comma clause stop
clause stop clause conjunction clause comma clause stop clause comma clause stop
clause comma dependant clause stop *before the networks played 24/7*
tab clause coordinator clause stop clause semicolon clause stop clause comma clause stop
clause question clause colon *Space-time is:*

      bullet noun *a haiku,*
a comment bullet noun
      bullet noun *a moment* *where meaning and symbol*
                               is briefly fused, then lost again.

tab clause exclamation clause comma clause conjunction solidus conjunction clause stop
clause (stop) clause conjunction clause comma clause stop clause comma clause stop clause
bracket noun comma noun comma noun comma noun comma noun bracket clause stop
clause year en dash year comma clause (stop) clause comma *thus language cannot be patented,*

tab quotation clause coordination clause (question comma) clause stop quotation
         center en dash italic title first name second name
a sign shifts through wormholes of meanings, one second to the next.
clause noun hyphen noun stop clause em dash clause em dash clause *latin* ellipsis
I guess that makes shared understanding an uncommon ground:
       two poles are never meeting.
[fig. 2] reading critical theory

It is amazing that anyone can communicate

anything at all.

The hubble telescope takes pictures of our universe. Galaxies are snapshots of big bang dots, like snow, like pixels, like white noise that follows the end of a TV broadcast

Green Tea Popsicles
Mary Rogers-Grantham

This is the year to fall in love with Earth,
choose paper at the grocery checkout,
and leave the plastic for dog owners.

Joshua Liquor sells potato bread on Fridays,
the Tea Cup opens at five every morning,
and Esther's Winery stays open until midnight.

This is the year to make green tea popsicles,
make martini yogurt and use nonfat milk,
and bring peace to your digestive system.

This is the year to obey flashing stop signs.

That Moment You Were Mistaken for Someone Else
Colin James

You were minding your own business
pandering to another dimension,
subsisting on mice and crickets.
I saw the large car approach
like a familiar dream.
The window rolled down.
Inside, quizzical looks then laughter.
You gave them an unburdened smile,
your usual comment on the peripheral.

A Coffin Covered with Wildflowers
Howie Good

1
We were fighting
the Indians in Florida.

You said a joke
without a punchline

isn't a real joke.

Why I always carry
an arrowhead in my pocket,

I said.

2
Thoreau passed
over the hill.

He only came out
when there was

a fire downtown.

3
The tall ships
of the China trade

returned bleeding.
A sign of something,

like a face shaded
by a wide hat.

i/dentity
Aimee Herman

ab   NORMAL
one hundred sit-ups per day   FLATTENS THE IT AWAY

:call me deviation.   .,<} /\| 00---{}

inter   SEX
between legs a fist rises   MUTINY

:When (I) was six, (I) tore out a section of my neck where the label
sat. where the label rubbed. where the label pushed pink where there
was yellow. where the label reconstructed [my] structure. where the
label took away sensation. where the label told {me} how to pee.
where the label disguised {me}. Disguised {me}. Discussed {me}.
DISgusts {me}.

inside on the   OUTSIDE
there is outside   INSIDE

:micro penis.   instru/MENtal

small formation like   INDECISION
color will cure it   FOR NOW.

:these sensations are not acceptable/inaccessible/the swelling/
                                          swallowing/
(I) looked {me} up in the book of explanations and found
                    graffiti'd pout/magnification of gen.i.tals

morph   OLOGY
bi   OLOGY
gender is not   SEX.

:doctor gave {me} a passport to cross the border of this body/man in
badges and nametag stopped {me} at the fringe of internal & external/
pouring of salt to/preserve **IT**/melt **IT**/embarrass **IT** away

:she/he/she/he/she/he/   ititititititititititititititititititititit

            fuck.

ambiguous   to doubt   debate   vague   (a) lie.

:just   call   me   a   question   mark.

defect.
dissect.
(lineage begins where incision

Green Lights/Purity of Vision
Kyle Muntz

Blue

A blue light is shining on the world. I wonder.

::::::::::::::::::::::

There's a girl who lives on my street. She spends her days playing violin and drinking water. When she weeps, the water leaves her body as tears, to be collected by the sky, until eventually that falls again as rain. Other times, she dances: slowly, as though worried she might fall, even with a floor there to catch her. Supervenient course, a wheel spinning in common. The present becomes an abrogated state.

A mist forms around her as she plays. The violin weaves golden streaks in it, of a subtly different shade, to diffuse in gentle increments, winding bands in it, cyphering inscriptions. Later, she sets the violin on top of her piano, and begins to play that. It lifts with a motion entirely her own. It tumbles.

At night, she sleeps. In the morning, she wakes. She eats water. Downcast eyes observe without seeing: nothing lives in the world, so there is nothing to see. Her room is quiet; only she breathes in it. She sits. She plays music. The light is blue. Her room has no windows. Only she can see.

I wonder.

::::::::::::::::::::::

Blue light crawls over the street when I look out my window; blue light hangs heavy in the curtains when they move, when I part them. The sidewalk is made of steps and stones, that people walk on, with routine benches in it, beside buildings, and spots for light, when you can find them. People sit in the benches, and look out windows. Occasionally I watch them—that must be obvious, or I wouldn't know they were there.

That blue light is muffled as the curtains close, elongating formations, making them darker. My room contains a table, a bed, a window, and me. And water. Every day, I go swimming; excepting that, there is very little to do, so I swim often, drifting. In blue water. The world is only one color. Every morning, I look into the sky, hoping to see the sun rise. But no, there is only the moon.

::::::::::::::::::::::

I'm not sure how it happened, but I'm writing about other people.
Is that possible? I never.
There are so many.

::::::::::::::::::::::

Mr. B is a pilgrim, eating pistachios—all this, proceeding from the discovery of saxophones (and language). If ever, to know the world as upholstery. Wherever he goes, he is listening to music: on the streets, in parking lots, on top of buildings, in concert halls, department stores. He carries his record player and a chair on his back: mobility
Look at this, he said, holding out a foreign object. Look closely.
What is it?
It has words in it.
Imagine that.
Do you know what they do?
I never.
When you look at them, they make things.
Like what?
Not pictures.
I scoffed. That's impossible.
Encapsulating scribbled light. Despite nonexistent objects. Semantic figures violate the universe.
I wonder.

::::::::::::::::::::::

Do you see me?
There was a girl in my room. She sat up on my bed; curtains of light wrapped around her like part of the moon. Her face in shadow, her figure negated. The window stared, admitting blue light.

A little.
Is that good enough for us? Are we visible here?
Just enough to matter, I said. Just enough to see.

::::::::::::::::::::::

Mr. B lives in a house without doors or windows; instead of walls, it has bookshelves, except really it has both, just they do different things, in different places, and they aren't shaped the same. Against one wall, it's easy to see a picture of a pyramid; old men with bald heads and golden rings rule its world, lifting all the weight of dead planets, to ride a chariot amongst cosmic fields, germinating stars... beneath that pyramid is a river, fed by some far mountain, cloaked in seasons of ice, whose atoms and participles are galaxies, black holes and expanding spheres: stillness, silence, and weight rivaled only by conceptual models of infinity, spoken but never seen, not with functioning eyes; absolution to decry exonerated space; an endless negation, unperceived.

My house is haunted, Mr. B told me.

By what?

Ghosts and shadows. Not in that order.

Any idea why?

He put on his detective cap and started smoking a pipe.

A long time ago, he said, *a family of kangaroos were murdered here. By accident, raccoons defiled the grave. Then a plane crashed into them. That plane was carrying*

the president;

a foreign minster;

his concubine;

three musicians;

their girlfriends;

a veterinarian;

a panda;

an interior designer;

somebody who made wigs;

and a bunch of other people without names.

Mr B paused to take a deep breath. *Later, skeletons began walking. They have voices but no vocal cords. Isn't that fantastic?*

I looked around. My neck hurt.

How did you get this place?

One day, he said, *when I was going somewhere, I found it. The door was open; it asked me to come in. I got my things, put them places, and made a sandwich. I've been here ever since.*

Oh, I said. *That makes sense.*

That day, in the street, I thought I saw a skull in the mist. It scowled, spat green flame, and began to wail. Like everything else, its surface shone a dull blue.

All its teeth had been sharpened to points.

::::::::::::::::::::::

Sometimes I pause to consider the things I say. I am aware, to some extent, of what it means to hear them: assimilation without context (extrovert semantic faculties), subject to whatever autocratic mechanisms. I suppose that makes them difficult to believe—but if anything, I think it's important to remember the nature of language itself. Everything I say is prefigured by an attribute of the world around me. Remember: I understand what it means to listen; I hear every word before I speak it; and I, myself, have no difficulty believing.

::::::::::::::::::::::

A naked girl lives in my room. She floats suspended before the window; the moon makes her glow. When I call to her, she appears to me. She is beautiful in the sense that light is beautiful.

I have a reason to be this way, she said.

I believe you.

Time passed. It still moved, even though I couldn't see it. Always and ever. Before.

When you consider existence, she considered, *aren't you ever afraid it will end?*

All the time.

Isn't that frightening?

You came to me out of the sky, I said. *When you reach out your hands, you can cup the moon.*

That isn't enough for me.

There's nothing to be afraid of, except nothing; and that doesn't exist, so there's no reason to be afraid of it.

If you can think of something—she looked up, through the ceiling—

it exists. At least in your mind, which is the only way that matters. Don't you remember?

We don't have to be the same. Not all the time.

Nothing changes, she said. *Everything exists, but nothing changes.*

To philosophize is to be defeated, more surely than a thing begins; we rolled in a glass orb defeated. A singularity amidst nothingness and water—what world is obscured, to be simply continued?

Our only thought occurred once, forever ago, to be endlessly remembered.

::::::::::::::::::::::::

I saw Mr. B outside a restaurant selling top hats and coffee. He sat in his chair, reading a newspaper.

Hello, I said.

Look over there. He pointed. *Do you see her?*

What?

That woman has an umbrella. She's hitting someone with it.

Wow.

Yeah, I know, there's blood.

It'll be alright though—her arm should get tired soon. Probably.

This is a sick world, he said.

I agree.

We're sick, he said, *but there's no one to take our temperature. We're freezing; the ice is coming soon.*

He was right; I needed a sweater.

::::::::::::::::::::::::

The world froze.

In the morning, when I got up, I would open the window to knock the icicles away; then I would make breakfast, and drink coffee; but I couldn't swim, because my water was frozen. Ice had taken over my room: the entire universe was a gigantic crystal, with bright shining lights in it, of coldness. In this great solid, there was no room for movement, no energy. Brushing my teeth was nearly impossible.

All day, wearing clothes, I huddled beneath blankets. My breath froze: first a mist, then a mass of droplets that fell like miniature hail.

Even shapes were breaking down, until everything was discombobulated geometry, within an immense solid.

I had forgotten to pay the heating bill.

::::::::::::::::::::::

On the streets, I saw a big group of people, all wearing thick coats with fur lining their faces, pulling treasure chests attached to heavy chains. They were everywhere— sidewalks, rooftops, the middle of the road— all moving slowly, almost like zombies; but I could see the breath as it encircled their bodies, misting just barely, so I knew they were alive: each with head down, back bent, shoulders forward, dragging a treasure chest. It was impossible to know where they were going. Even if I were to ask, I doubted I would receive an answer.

::::::::::::::::::::::

After much effort, I thawed my room.

I'm not proud of the things I did to accomplish this.

(I got a job carrying a flamethrower around the city, melting people.

My coworkers treated me like shit.)

::::::::::::::::::::::

Like a kid, I jumped down a hill—almost in a sled, except the sled was my body—to slide: an immense inverted landscape, falling hundreds of feet. At the base, breathing hard, I decided I really wanted a cup of coffee. When I stood to get it, somebody (wrapped so I couldn't see their face) came up and tackled me; and didn't get off. If I hadn't pushed him, I might have been buried in the snow.

What was that about?

I'm not going to describe quite what happened, but by the time I got him to stop, the other guy had a branch stuck in his abdomen. He must have been afraid to take it out, because he just looked at it, and wiggled the end a bit.

Revenge, he replied.

For what?

I can't tell you, because it hasn't happened yet.

I think you've got the wrong person.

That isn't possible, he replied. *In all the world, there's only one of you; and right now, this is where you are. So it can't be anyone else.*

From some direction that wasn't ours, wind blew. A mandala of leaves let fall copious teardrops of blue snow

The bottom of the hill was a thought and a place and a color. It had two people and a bunch of trees in it.

You should probably get that looked at. I pointed at his stomach. *Sorry, I guess. Even though it's your fault.*

This is nothing, he groaned. *Just a flesh wound.*

Still, you're bleeding.

Someday, he said, *I'll get you.*

I scratched my chin. *You sound like somebody else.*

What?

It's nothing, don't worry about it. I waved my hand. *Get out of here. You might get eaten by a bear.*

That's ridiculous. There aren't any bears around here.

I'm not so sure. Behind him, I saw the flaming skeleton of an animal, hideously thin, extending its claws; and above that, yes—its eyes glowing green, drool frozen around its mouth—the head of a bear. No mammoth sounds of it; there are fields in this country. Each field we pass smells of sewage and cranberries.

::::::::::::::::::::::

I was walking through the inside of a school and met Mr. B there too—I could tell it was him because I could hear really loud jazz from down the hall, miles outside the building. Today he'd brought a table with him. He was reading a manual about how to dissect octopuses, a treatise on the nature of matter, and Proust (as rewritten by someone rewriting Borges—who might, therefore, have been Borges himself).

There are already enough Frenchmen in the world, he said. *In France.*

Somebody walked outside the room, holding their ears, which had begun to bleed. I wondered if they would be deaf, later. Mr. B and I had a short conversation about aquatic animals and quantum mechanics, yelling every word.

You were right, I said, *about the weather.*

What do you expect? He laughed. *The sky can only go so long without a sun.*

::::::::::::::::::::

The naked girl took a bath, whirled in steam. Her shoulders faced me. Because of the bathtub, I couldn't help noticing that her skin was the color of porcelain—and for the first time in the history of words, it was finally true.

What do you think? she asked, turning. *When I reflect the light like this, does it make me beautiful?*

Of course.

She lowered her eyes. *What are you thinking about?*

Snow shovels. When they have snow in them, they're really hard to lift.

Are you angry with me?

No.

You're lying, I can tell.

I told you before—you can stay as long as you want. It doesn't matter what happens.

To the world?

It can take care of itself, I said.

I'm destroying it.

I repeated myself, but I have no idea if she believed me. (I don't think so.)

::::::::::::::::::::

My life was bigger than a tower, a tall one—glass shining outwards—until somebody crashed a car into it, both in and through the windows (that person was myself; I was driving) to make broken, or fall; casting loose a shower of glass, inward flux of particles, impossibly sharp to the touch, glistening with icy water...the shards fell down, and down, and downward, until finally there was no more down, no lower place in all the world (because of its surface), and up above, in the shattered remnants of the highest building, I was looking at myself, face tilted like the sky, on the verge of shutting my eyes, seeing only when I glanced out through them, which wasn't often, watching this world, all a single color.

Up in the sky, the moon began to move; I couldn't believe it.

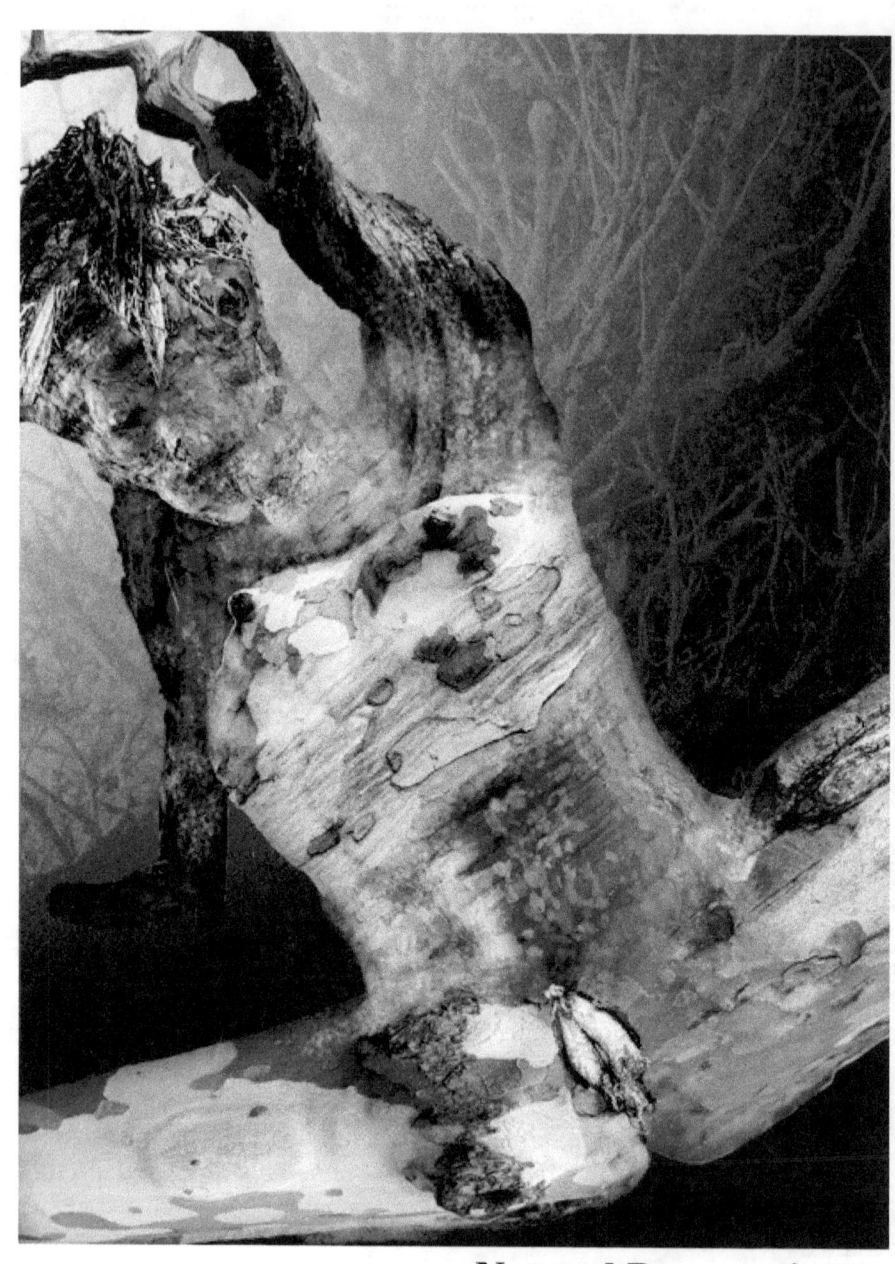

Natural Provocation
Antoine Monmarché

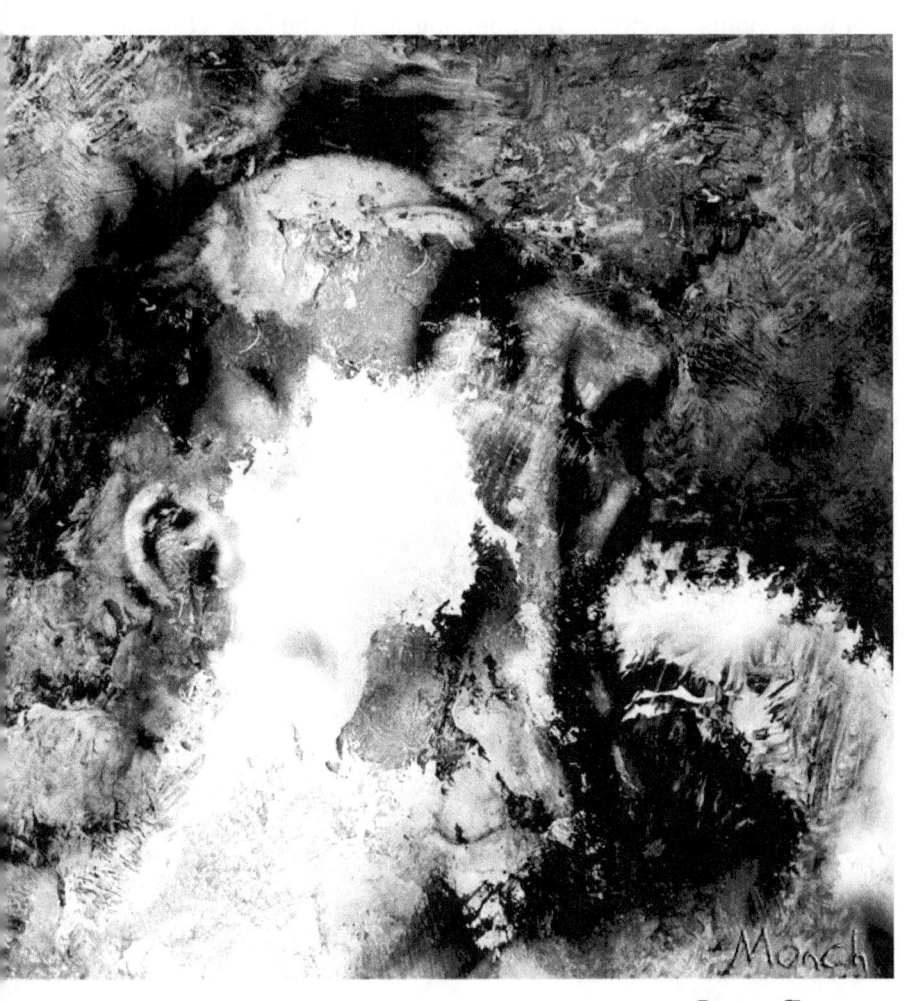

Overflow
Antoine Monmarché

what the woman at the retro bar said
Mark L.O. Kempf

I was helping gravity with a troubling stool at the new retro-bar,
Hotel de Boutique Folle,
drinking what amounts to Absinthe these days. This woman,
too-thin, near shorn with a silver-lace party dress was somehow
keeping her bomb-red gloss on, entertaining three guys and two,
well, just babes, like four-year-olds at a library puppet show.

She was too devastatingly exotic a kitten to not hear meow.
I slunk over to the quorum on the pretext of reloading,
carefully keeping my back to hers, and waited. She spoke,
in a silk, Parisian accent demure – within five she began
this slight lean, so her back, then her ass, would touch me,
somehow in an unmistakable orderly pattern,
a rumba extracted from hi-drunken voices.

Later on, much later on, upstairs, room six-oh-five, lounging
till she's ready for a nightcap, leaning till hot breath and breasts
touch me triste murmure brisé;

I thought you were Michelangelo's David turns out,
you're Paolo Malatesta.
Come here Rodin.

I love a woman who can kiss with jazz like that playing in her head.

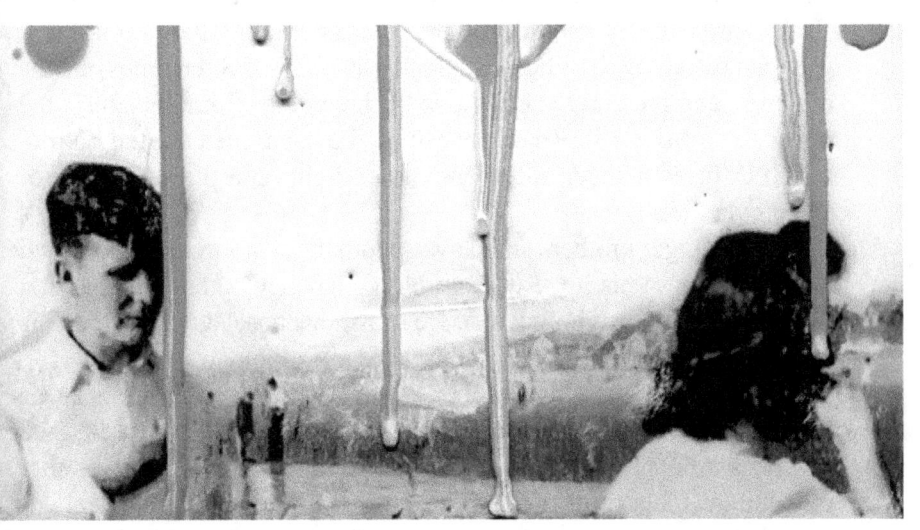

Memory #5
James Short

The Reason Why
Thomas Gough

The reason why made the younger brother holler. The banks of long-ago dynamited rock and the black shapes of trees on top of the banks of long-ago dynamited rock took his voice and swallowed it, and so the younger brother stopped walking, and, in the center of the gravel road, he cupped his hands to his mouth and shouted again. This time his words returned, trailing high up in the wet branches of the trees, high enough that he turned to the sky, as if it were responsible. The sky was cloudy, closed, and thin strings of rain fell out of it, but it was also lit. Not by city-light or streetlight—he was three miles outside of Davis, and probably another two or three miles from his house, the next one on Mine Hill Road—but lit by the bona fide celestial bodies, which diffused a sheen of green-colored light onto the little pane of cloud over him.

The younger brother turned away from the sky, lurched, and tasted the salt again on his lip. Salt from blood, he knew, though he had not seen himself and had no wish to. He turned his nose again, slapped his cheeks. Nothing was broken and the cold even took away the sting.

Always with the older brother it was why. The older brother was ten years older, and the younger brother thought of that time as the why years. Pondering, pondering, pacing back and forth in the shitty little hut the older brother called his studio while his children went un-schooled and ate snails. The younger brother stopped, laughed aloud at himself. This was a little story he was making, but for whom? For their mother, it occurred to him. So he would have something to complain about when she praised the older brother during their phone conversations.

You've been living there free of charge for almost two years.

Free of charge? Is that what she thought? Wiping the ass of his nephew and listening to an eight-year-old hack away at the times tables while the older brother stood in his studio and pondered the reasons why? This was not free, it was inordinately expensive. Which brought him back to why, then, just like the older brother would have liked.

Why was he out here? the older had asked.

To live.

And why was he alive?

The younger brother looked into the dark pit of trees in front of him. Don't you fucking know? he thought. He was answering the older brother, revising a conversation they had finished last fall.

No, the older brother would likely have said, I don't know.

The younger brother made his way to the edge of the small, dark valley. He saw the tips of pine, heard the falling of unseen water, the gurgling and turning course of it in the dark. He had meant to throw up his hands and give his final answer on the subject of the lost conversation, but he felt his energy waning just then, and he took hold of a tree beside the road. When he did his arm trembled as it had hours ago during the fight. The sensation returned him to that moment, not to the details of it, since these did not matter, but to his body as he taken the first swing. He felt his arm coming home, the weight of his hand striking flesh. Down in the valley, some animal cried out.

There you go, he said to his older brother. There's your reason fucking why.

Strength in Numbers
Frank Roger

Help!

They're after us 418, and they're 17 everywhere 6839. No doubt we 52 walked straight into an 428 ambush here, and we're 276 trapped without 442 a chance of escape 36847.

671 Can anyone 49873 hear us? Please help us 45822 before it's 6673 too late! 8992 55367 In a few more minutes 887 4759 66 231 these goddamned numbers 18 27 will have us 457 8842 3795 by the throat 574 88 634.

56 2387 I always 33 697 152 detested 447 88567 numbers 18 812 663, only now they appear 8796 54711 to return the feeling 447 8967 21305. 5047 Of course, 447 I don't want 7887 96 to generalise 66 324. We're dealing 777 12 with radical elements here 45786 11 257, fundamentalist numbers 012 3668 14 that are out to turn all non-numerical beings 879 9963 399 into zeroes 77 8125 36 9845. In 457 23 their opinion 45587 99 we've probably 114 254 33687 been 159 444 zeroes 587 213 all along 00 2458.

124 000 2547 845 62 Dammit 144 23! They've 457 0000 5487 surrounded us 457 899 657 0000 245! We 457 88 457 don't stand 000 2457 63 a chance 547 against them 00 233!

142 54 0000 3655 If no one 44578 00 2567 00 out there 15 000 243 87 acts 4578 99 000 11 quickly the 788 000 5476 battle will be lost 178 000 2547! Doesn't 155 000 36 anyone hear 445 us then 16 000 2354 78? 1254 Or has 45 000 3689 77 everyone 458 00 236 5547 yielded already 4457 000 544 791 to the superior 114 4578 000 88712 numbers 496 360 000 578 and 47 8996 been reduced 4578 166 350012 to a 4578 12 000 36 bunch of 4578 absolute 4475 000 36 547 zeroes 789 000 36 7845 9924 0000?

447 000 238 79 Too late 4578 00 2322 771! It's 4458 00 too 457 88 90036 late 457 80097 now 5478 88 000 235 46! 4578 Our 14 000 3677 final 55 000 367 attempt 477 7003 6800 21 at putting 212 000 587 up a fight 4779 0336 77 led 6632 000 8953 to 77 8002 45000 639 nothing 8777 0000 513 9596 22.

000 211 568 It's 557 000 over 6887 18 6661 for 124 000 367 us 7781 0000 25 now 544 7007 24 61. 45 88888 40025 997 I suppose

5502 74 the numbers 000 236 554 2970 made 886 0000 457 6012 380 it 333 25 000 471. 255 23 Dammit 799 000 541 83!

87 5411 000 23 We've 111 475 000 5036 been 87046 11 reduced 000 477 806 to 447 2601 7809 zeroes 773 0000 5407 9610 23 550.

887 000 2658 994 0245 8978 000125 547852 zeroes 875497 8521 0025 4578 1023 60124 5501 25478 6325 44 7850 2534 0000 5421 5878 6524 3012 778 54218 0000 24587 22 3245 874 00124 5874 21036 250014 547 77784 024 5801 205 475 000 5463.

754 700 254 8745 0000 54 70236 25487 23 0000 54872 7 245 336 0000 2145 78047 542 30210 25746 0000 2365 554036 210145 225 787 554 0000 125 9669 11 2366 0000 257 808 9780 3365 0152 00 547 555 864 1203 557 889 997 5458 22403 0000 2547 8874 2236 5552 00000 45788 89741 2354 0000 2547 5558 78554 00000 2410 236 5054 20005 5587 445 66687 00000 5547 8887 241 0213 5403 225 999 547 000 24 54006 587 9965 300214 57 45 33 6587 2540 1204 22 20214 22 0000 4478 557 505 5012 20036 285 0000 114 7777 96003 87 874 588 444 2000 1254 0000 2202 3677 8987 222 0000 2458 0000 000 55 347 11 7 18 0000 30 03 1957.

Rain, Dance
Jeffrey Alan Russell

Cold-face drops of rain-
Drum circles while munching burritos,
watching you fall into the shape of rams,
fingers lingering on blades of grass.

Weathered flags and easterly winds,
giving way to the smell of the hoo-ha man--
limiting my flurry of emotions--
while you crept on your belly.

"Come on, we got the world" she says,
tip toe, tip toe,
swinging around with her arms,
held so smoothly by arches.

Folding into my chest,
she, music, held close—
all at the same time,
dancing, falling slightly.

Reading the bottom of her feet,
I followed through the spider-web—
sticky, stuck, blind,
going for too much,
lick-spill.

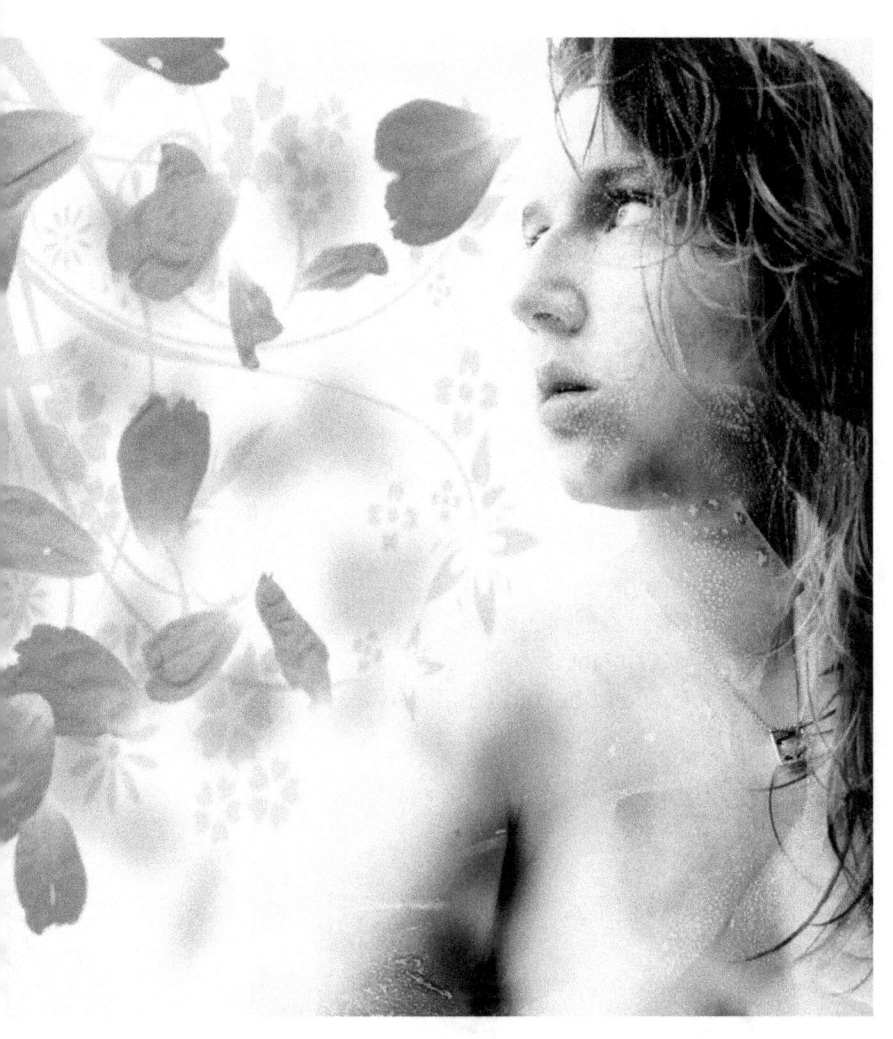

I Used to Fall in Love
Matt Parsons

Approbations 682
(after Mark Turner's "Water Stones")
Felino A. Soriano

Sub
-merged

                    full near noon's boiling over symptom
amid innate thrust of cooling hearsay
        subjective tolerance
                        until
overwhelming juncture promotes
aspectual need to shed

        angled heat
                more so collocated
                       with hyperactive promis-
sory
           hope than
hankering to divide dried circumference of sound
with magnetic spontaneity
harboring pinnacle of devoid familiarity.

Approbations 695
(after Miles Davis' "Circle")
Felino A. Soriano

Drawn by
hand
           by imagination's apathetic hand.
Semiotic motional
meaning
     dense exploratory broken record
dominant contours of

existential fundamental betrayal. Of your mirror's
faceless evidence
         cycles of your name
reinterpret daily rituals
                open
toward excitation's tragedy
of
     otherness.

Lani and Hyde
Tanner Almon

After winning a whopping $77 at Bingo night, Lani cheerfully rides the bus home to share the news with her boyfriend, Hyde. They quickly blow the money on some lottery tickets that unfortunately are not winners. Not knowing what else to do they decide to rob a thrift store... again. Because their previous attempt at robbing Value Village had not ended so well they decide to up their game by wearing disguises. They go about this by quickly stealing some short shorts and tube socks from American Apparel. Now, disguised as sexy hipster models, they are able to easily slip into Value Village unnoticed and pocket several vintage toys. Once outside the store they suddenly realize that they have no bus money or getaway car, so Hyde calls his mom, who reluctantly gets out of bed and into her station wagon. Once back at what Hyde likes to refer to as his "Man-Cave", Lani and Hyde put on a show with some of their loot while Hyde's mom photographs the various "goings-ons." Some of the more family friendly photos are shown here.

Behind-the-Scenes:

Unfortunately for Lani and Hyde, several of the photographs taken that night by Hyde's mother were later used against them on a gripping episode of Judge Judy. Fortunately for Lani and Hyde, the Judge Judy appearance led to a lucrative reality show where each week they would break into celebrity homes and steal whatever pets they could find.

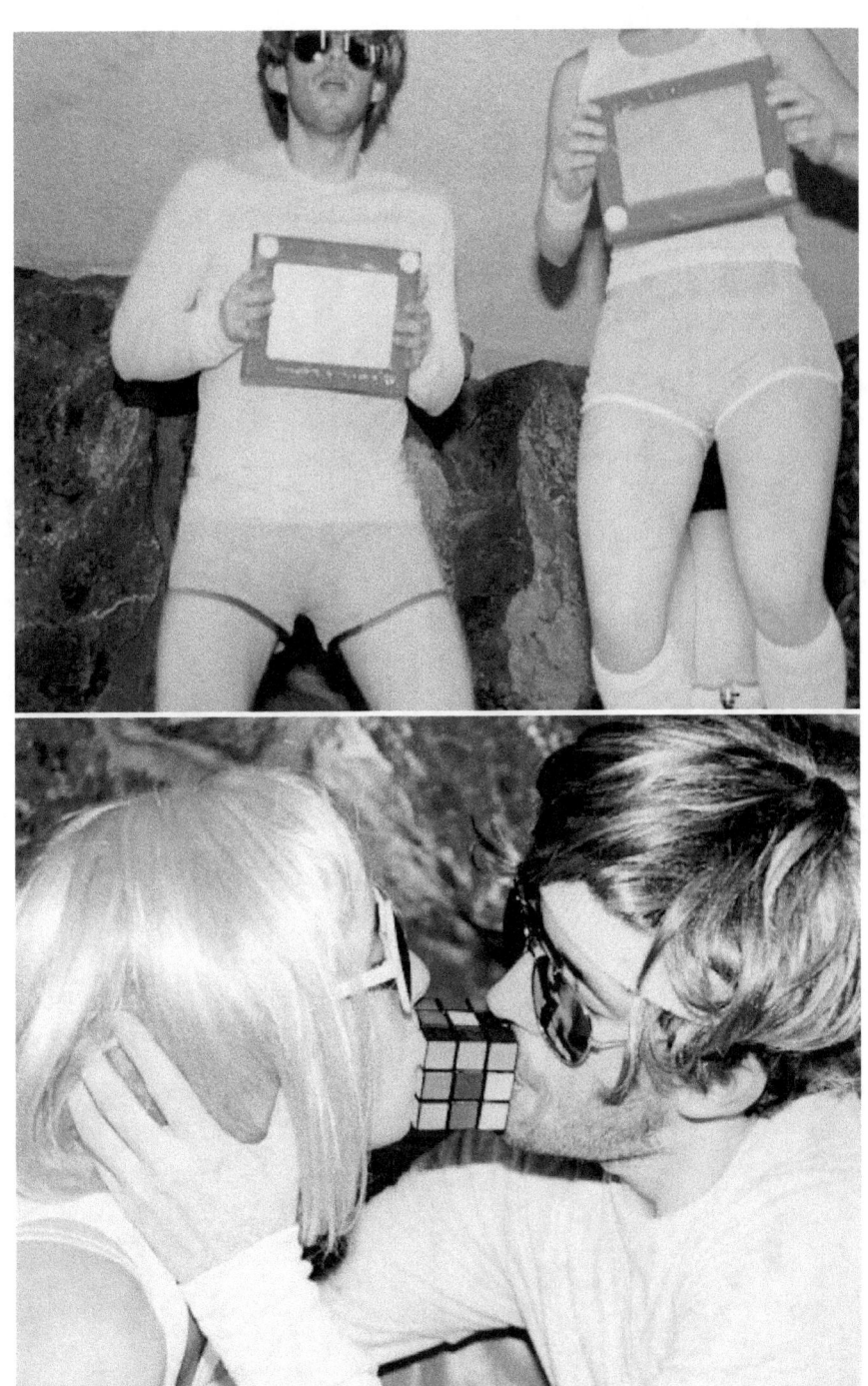

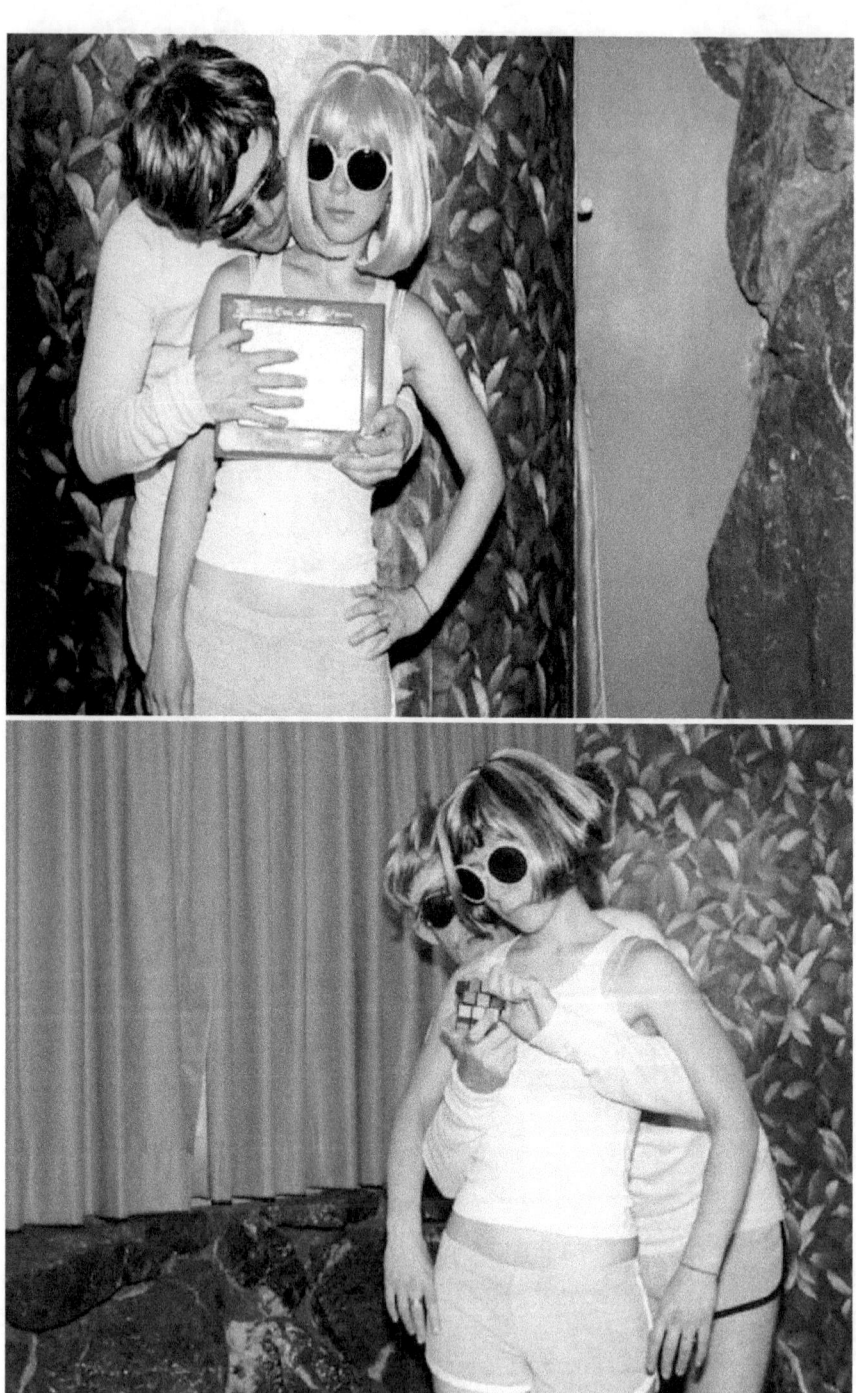

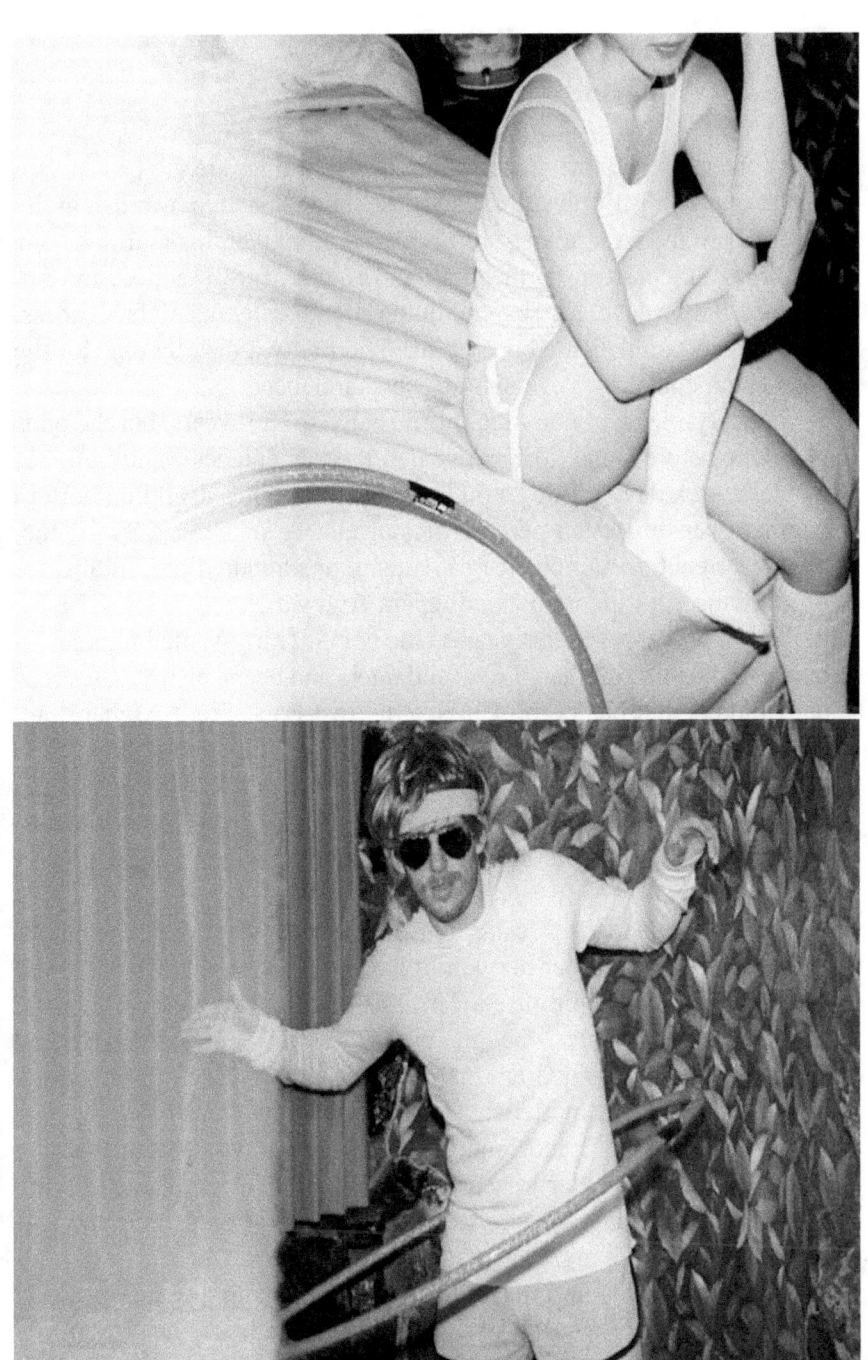

Wednesday Morning Rodeo
Michael Andreoni

You have breakfast in the bathroom if mornings are too fast and apt to slip away. It isn't pleasant; cup of tea in one hand, hair brush in the other. Keep them far apart—you can at least do that this morning? she inquired of the mirror. Permed hair and oolong...gross. Stroke and sip, bite of whole wheat toast, bare of butter or jelly after the night's excess, peasant food on delicate bone china. Too pretty a dish by half for the soap-scum counter. "Yes you are," she announced.

Twenty-nine and counting, prime baby-spittin' years, but the odds were about to change. She marshaled the percentages easily; all that frontal cortex dust left by "You Go Girl" magazines. Children born to parents over thirty: ten percent greater chance of Downs Syndrome, twelve percent greater chance of Autism, one hundred percent chance of screwing your life up beyond repair. And yet....

But it was moot as last year's chic boots. Thirty-something men in bars, oh, the thrill of them. Lions and tigers and bears, oh my, sales reps and soldiers and clerks, oh Christ. Mr. Just-Back-From-Afghanistan, last night; forty-mile stare, G.I. Bill, death's head in dress blues. "The things I've seen," he whispered, clutching a handful of her ass on the dance floor. "I am not your mommy," she sang to the mirror while out-lining eyebrows. Too old for mid-week clubbing—there, she'd thought it. Now what?

Climb the ladder of desire. A corner office with windows and all those comely men under her would have to do what she wanted. And she would want, she promised. The glass ceiling was already cracked, if not broken, by others, though. Where was the challenge? Kick and claw to V.P. of Boring Crap, manage that 401K—HEY! "The golden age of Wymen," she muttered. "Thanks for all that."

The sneaky Y chromosome...fooled us good. All those men acting like they have a wonderful secret: exciting jobs, lives fulfilled, living off the fat of the land. Where was it? Did it exist? Sales reps and sol-diers and clerks, oh my; all lies.

The toast was gone and good riddance. Touch up the hair now, gild the lips; blot and blow. Rope was what she wanted, just then. A cosmic lariat to lasso the possibilities; tie 'em up and brand 'em—they'd all be hers. Pick and choose and cull. Snap that whip.

The mirror pronounced her ready but she lingered, examining all the details. Giants had created her, she knew; tore their bridles off one by bloody one across centuries to bequeath this agony of choice. That she might have the whip in her hand instead of on her back.

Every kick of their rebellion scored her flanks, though, blows upon bruises, the effect calculated long before: To turn her, turn her from the corral, she knew, and celebrated it. But her sister's expectations weighed heavily, made it hard to turn in her own direction. She saw the gate rushing at her from out of the mirror and knew at last the trap had been set by men and women both. "But I don't have to do it their way," she challenged. I'll spit the bit and round on 'em all. Buck 'em off. Take their reigns. YANK. I know what to do now. Saddle up, saddle up, saddle up.

Now… let's just assume it's out there waiting, she exulted, that bronc of a hundred destinies. Let's act like we know it's there and plunge out of the gate ready to rope. A last glance into the mirror, car keys jingling like spurs. Now ride 'em, ride 'em hard.

Ping Pong Divorcing Knocks
Ricky Massengale

it's ping pong
a person on each   side
                              by themselves
            and the rubber padding has been ripped
                                                            or torn
leaving the hard slug trail to r,i,p,p,l,e, the lights
                              which t[(w)o]o
                                                  fli-
                                                        cker
knick   .   .   .   knock
          knick   .   .   .   knock
          but the ball gets lower   gains
                                        speedfaster
knickknock   sounds
like fighting   and the ball goes faster
                  speeding:
            jesus and zeus pingponging the moon
[. . .]
then there are four
two of a person on each side
togethernowone
            holy matrimony with commitment on each finger and the
lovin(g)leam in eyes as they casually nod to one another, only for his
hand to grasp her shoulder in comfort and their eyes to turn down as
they watch the other side with its own two of a person
            knickknocking now . . .
knockknickingknickingknock--   knock
          "why this way?"
"NET BALL!" (breathingsmiles of one of the twoed one) "and this--
                              7 serving six--"
"years of"
          "divorce"
"not marriage"
          "and seven years"

"of not our"
        "but"
"our marriage," and another hand to drape the narrow should
(knick) -er   (knock) (knick)(knock)
[. . .]
knockingknickingknockingknicking
                                8 serving 8 years of
                                pain cars money
not children food memories smiles frowns
                                but new
smiles, new
frowns, new
comfort, new
2 of 1's, new
mr(s).'s
knockknick . . .
(drawing hand) (tension) . . .
        & smac(k)nick! into   an-
                                other of a their
unrubbermattedwoodenpaddles

then, the ball flies, bounces
        harder
and now they all stand by the net,
 (knocking)
        (knicking)
    (knocking)
--ball in air--
--they swing, four of--
--two--
to knock
        (not on the child's door
or knick   his height
butyou'reagrowingboy
on the doorframe but
there's the frame with
the paint they brushed
with oncetogether shoulders

```
[ . . . ]
2p                                                    2p
a                          ball                        a
 d                        stalled                      d
 d                    rolling in air        d
 l                         still                        l
 e                         stuck                        e
 s                                                      s
          in                             the
                  middle          the
four meet for
the ball
which falls
crushed
[ . . . ]
net falls

drapes

smashed ball

that they gaze at, it likened to their eye, a pale coin.
```

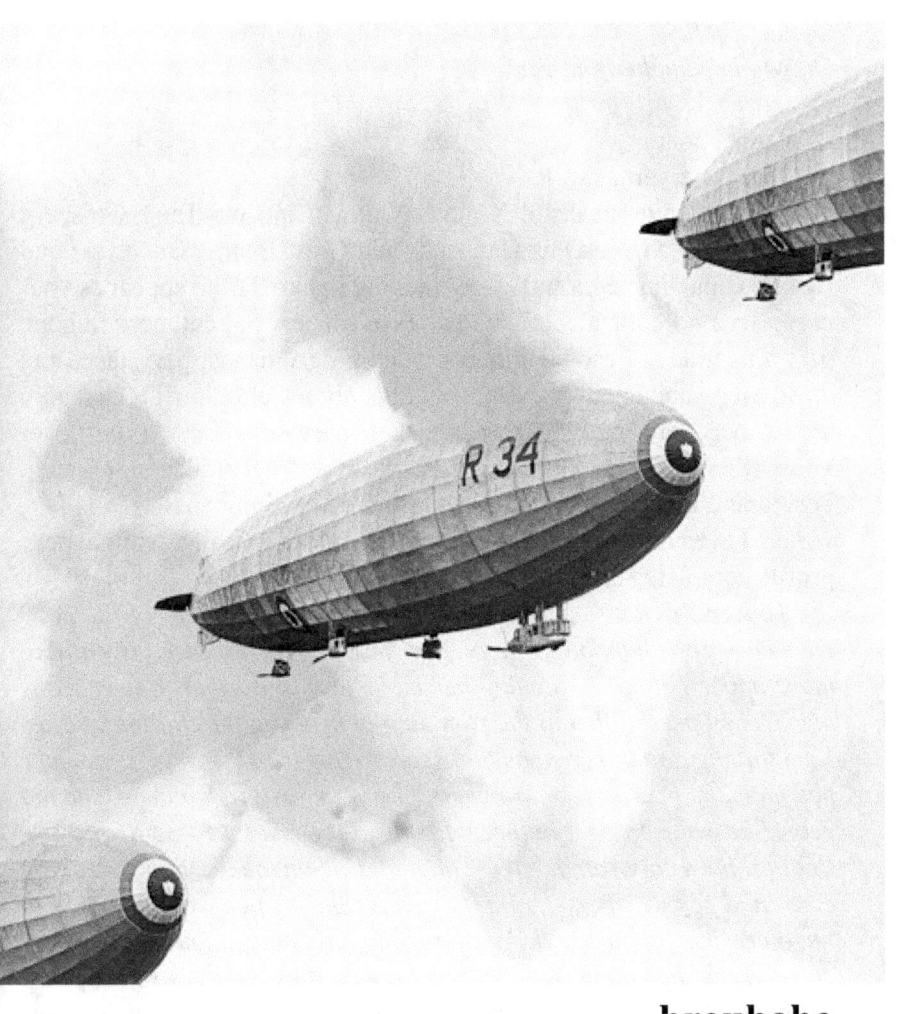

brouhaha
James Short

Just Trying to Get You to Wonder about Who You Fear
Echezona Udeze

I will dream an infinity
Of make believe
Only to be caught up in you

I am a poet.

I am a pervert as well.

My language speaks of X-men, Whitman and Wu-Tang, Ginsberg and Giovanni, Green Day, Gangstarr and Grey, Beatty, Bukowski and Beatlemania, Fugee La and finger fucking Lauryn Hill. I appear as your normal perv. I collect comic books. I have a perv haircut, perv fingers, perv fingernails, perv teeth, perv weight, perv hands, perv face, and those ever watching perv eyes. I wear perv brand clothing. I rock a perv t-shirt, perv hat, perv shoes, perv jeans, perv sunglasses, (you never know where), perv socks, perv underwear, and perv calculator watch. Perv brand clothing ... 'get some loser.' Everything about me is perverted. I even collect comic books, superhero specifically. Normal perv profile complete and noted.

I invent, quick step, quick step. She is what I dream of for now. Heaven with a handbag, the picture of beauty. And there is nothing more important than watching her move at this moment. Her grace is my passion personified in the stomping of heels, in the shifting of hips. I am finding god in her steps that seem to linger in the air. I remember her face, the rest is mine to invent. She is an art grad student, second year. She wants to do it in three. In music she loves Neo-Soul, and The Beatles, hard core rap like Wu-Tang, and TV on the Radio, Paul Simon circa and post Garfunkel, and it extends. She is open wild terrain with huge crevices naturally deep. She is my city, and ... she caresses my cheek. I feel her body's warmth meld with mine, waist is soft. I place my hand at her side. Enjoy the sun rising in the center of her iris. She asks me how I am doing. I do not answer. I kiss her, and again, and again, and again as my answer. She has solved my problem. Our hands rest lazily in a cradle position. She presses up against me tight. I inhale her humidity, her split ends, kiss her round, her cheek. Her huge brown

eyes blink and I am mad I did not look into them for a fraction of time.
This time is ours. This time is now. She tickles my fingertip with her
right hand. Let's her hair down with her left. To god goes the glory for
letting her be. For letting her be here. For letting her be here with me.
I kiss her again. While her toes play with my ankle. Our feet wrapped
up like a cat in twine. She makes my brain more than tingle. She shines.
Light embraces me. Holds on tight without lifting a finger. My hands
slide across the curve of her belly and hips. The curve of her mind when
I ask her how she is doing. She replies by kissing me again and again
and again. Her bottom lip is a little moist after she playfully bites my
cheek. I suck it dry. Press the palm of her hand.

Then we begin. Begin body speak. Auras with the same glow
rolling up. Her gravitational pull destroys everything you thought you
knew.

And the crowd
Cried out sicko
While he Dreamed
of joining them
But they believed
The words shouted
And he stood there
Struggling to disbelieve
Struggling to disprove
And struggling
To be himself

We step higher and higher until she goes inside to get a cup of coffee and my fantasy trip has ended. FIN.

There is a banner in the window of this coffee shop that says 'Jesus
Saves,' black lettering on a white canvas. WWJD? I stare at her and my
reflection at the same time and know she will not be my savior, more
Magneto than anything. Tears build, still I walk away smiling, then
the dark circumvents. It is everywhere. This dark to myself is me and
you and everything, it is unnamable, it is a force. Don't trust the force.
Similar to the bloodlust or whatever pop culture craze is the flavor of
the week. I look around for a local bathroom to jack off in and I find the
solace of her kisses in my imagination. Her kiss is all I missed.

The banner Jesus saves shined
While they threw me off a cliff
into reality

I beat off with the hurt weighing in my heart since I know it is all about that one girl. The princess high in the tower, the woman I cannot have. In the end always an ice queen. The one I will yearn for forever. Every woman I invent is a slight variation of this woman and I cannot let her go. She controls my dreams, has controlled them since the seventh grade when she said, "hello ... is it me you're looking for."

After the crowd said goodbye
She said hello
And nothing else ever mattered

Jubilation Lee light surrounds me when I enter my dreamscape, day or night. While I am fantasizing her light splits my eyes wide awake. The sun wakes up in the morning and greets you on this new day. Here comes the sun. Everything is naturally bright. But God snuffs out the sun when he sees we require rest. It finishes. I am once again solitary in this world where everything is dark.

I walk away wondering about the sign in the store window and I believe Jesus should have saved me a long time ago. I am still recovering from the blows Jesus gave my skull. The cut Christianity left along my right eye. And the Macho Man says this, the match was the impossible burden and still I am a virgin at 24 years of age. "Jesus can save, but can he get you laid." "No," I mumble to myself, "he's like pussy repellant." And the light returns as I round the corner, and isn't it inviting. The light is similar to the light that shined on me when I made up that girl. There is a light that shines. This place is the only bright spot in my life other than the creations I spin. Who doesn't want to go where everybody knows your name?

Outside of this place a group of people swarm with banners that say "Jesus Loves You" and "The Lord Heals." They pester me once I am visible. It seems they are trapped in a darkness in the middle of a normally bright afternoon. Some eyes are massive and blue while actually black holes. Some hair is stark blond but the strands are tainted with an invisible ugly. An ugly that seems to last an eternity. One woman whispers, "You can spot these sickos from a block away." Other snickers and giggles meet me like a frozen handshake but what they tell me is pure, Jean Grey pure. False love is showering me as if acid rain is pouring on my soul. They tell me god can save, god does love me, and I must join them in order to enter paradise. "Come and be saved," one spouts over the heads of the entire street. Filling the narrow paths of this world with darkness since the same woman snickered.

Can't she heal me?
You forsake me into life
And keep me from happiness
I'll go worship the devil
Since you don't give a shit

The sign flickers bright outside of le sex shoppe with the power of a million imploding suns. Your local pervs gather round and fantasize about the tail they are not and never will be having. The man behind the counter smiles when he sees me and greets me as the sun by what I have come to accept as my name: "Hey Schitzo Larry!"

"Hey Steve!"

I walk over to the TV where "it" is happening. A beautiful light fills the room. The way, the light. It dances and shifts. Bends and breaks into a thousand silver dollars littering my mind. The thing that seems forbidden to us is there for us to watch. "Looks like fun to all virgins," I think, "especially those that are 24 years old."

I invent while a content statue.

Hail her - hail beauty
I worship more than god
Through my prayer of you
I pray at the altar of carnality
Since we are animals in reality

Here you are welcome. Out there they do not care. Here you are accepted in the glow. Out there you are another 'lost soul.' Here you are respected. Out there they snicker. Here you are wanted. Out there you are nothing. Here it is light all day until closing time. Out there it is dark. Here you are a lonely person. Out there scum. Here you are needed. Out there another notch in god's big man's belt. Here is home. Here is home. Here is home.

This is the only place where I at least feel open. A gift is unwrapped, the bow pulled apart and the wrapping paper fragmented into tiny islands. I can talk here without those heavy judging eyes piercing what they believe is my heart.

Everything is illuminated here it dazzles like ultimate X-men. Especially that woman on the TV screen who I watch. While I begin to vertically incline a friend slides up to me.

"Hey Schitzo Larry ... how've ya been?"

"Randomly searching the aisles for love."

Lost in aisles of supposed sickness
My search ends
This world will not love me
This seeming sicko store
Is my safe haven

The darkness is once again delved into. Okay Alice, down the hatch or Rabbit hole or whatever pill you take. I am once again locked in a tight 10' by 10'cell, trapped in my own mind. At times it can seem I am beating the walls of my skull to break free, but I cannot. So I sit in my head and run from mice chasing me in my skull. I hit the streets and people stare as if they have just lost a hand. The stares I receive from women are not kind. They are judging me. And I find many to be beautiful. Some I invent to get through my day, but, I am a pervert. They are like striking of stone on stone. Creatures composed of lovely force me to think up the unexpected. A frosting break from the mundane. You Jim Carrey or something. They are the light in this dark hovel but I am a fly. I am blind without their direction. I spin madly from here to there to nowhere. Ignored or squashed my entire life. A ballaretic wolverine. Just a speck, nothing at all.

Saw Silence of the Lambs
Is there a perfect reflection
Of me in Hannibal
Or am I refracted images
of this world that hates me

At my apartment outside I more than pick up my roommates colossus proportioned pumping iron music and I am frustrated that 'sleaze ball' is even there. I crack the door and his roommate guffaws grotesquely, instantaneously in a dimly lit room.

And they all call me a perv
While his mind is warped to hell
I am all alone
He is doing swell

"What's up virgin – What's in the bag?"
"Fantasies, dreams, and beautiful visions."
"We have to get you laid, you're like a midget cyclops."
My roommate is highly touted by the opposite sex, at least in terms of datability. My roommate's porn collection totals 45 magazines and 75 DVD's. He converted from VHS last year. Mark's pornography is 400 percent that of mine but no woman considers Mark a pervert. He keeps it exquisitely well-hidden under his bed from the women in his life. A closet pervert, but we all are sick deep down inside. Most just know how to hide it better. Mark's also openly sexist, racist, snobbish, and a cheat. They can do bad by their damn selves.

And the pervert
decided
love was not here
nothing was but
his hand and lotion
the crowd then
began to jeer
as he beat off
with ferocity

I have come in numerous times and found Mark cheating on the woman he terms his 'main girl' when the others are not around. Legs in air, clothes tossed around, on the couch, in the open. He once paused in the middle of the deed and told me as if he possessed a drop of wit, "You should really try this one day."
But the women rolled in through a revolving door and they praised

him to the high heavens? He is handsome, well-employed, and drives a sports car. Is that what love is? Watching him I had almost lost all faith in romance, the opposite sex, karma, and most importantly love. I really wanted to connect, to bond like annoying knots with Mark's girlfriend.

And she is … the most amazing woman in the world to me, Jean Grey all day. The only one I feel I can talk to without feeling heavy judging eyes, and her eyes are black, her mind a sanctuary, her body my temple. She cared when all others just laughed at me and passed me off as a sicko. She is beautiful, but it's what sits inside her skull that I crave. Her warmth. Her compassion. Her care.

While I head to my room, she arrives, and I believe a million rose petals should be thrown at her feet. She stands at 5'7", with dark shoulder-cut hair, and a smile that never grins. Her smile is a contained nuclear explosion. Everything drops dead when she goes boom. Havoc takes over and worlds crumble to myself. Funny thing is she is also Christian. Her style speaks of modesty, block colors, cheap shoes, few accessories with little make up, slight splashes and natural rosy red tinted cheeks. Her lips I have never noticed, you must breathe in her face in one fell swoop. You must breathe her in to enjoy anything to me, anything worth mentioning. Her nose curves downward when she smiles and there is a hint of the devious. Not so thin, enjoys her plumpness in a two piece anywhere there is a large mass of water. She never blushes. Her movements and attitude are the epitome of freedom to me. She is the epitome of everything I desire in love and life. Jean Grey okay. Jean grey all day.

And to dream
of what can be
in you and me
are dreams of we

She smiles at both of us but kisses Mark. I linger for chit chat until Mark says, "go beat off or something." She shoots Mark the look. The Big Bully stops dead frozen and says, "what?"

This is why I love her.

"It's okay," I mumble, "I was headed out anyways, Anna." I jumble the few steps into his room and I invent.

And she is
Every fantasy trip
I have ever experienced
Tales of my self
Rescuing the princess
Comic book spins
Of a Superman going
Down the lane
My hero's journey
Condensed into soul
A true fairy princess
The ring I would never abuse
The only crown
I deserve to wear
Sits in you

'Hello.' 'Hello.' 'How are you.' 'Great now that you're here, Larry.' *She kisses me exactly like she kisses Mark and we then proceed to cuddle don't we. Then talk. Tell me what floats through that pretty mind. Tell me what you love and loathe, aspirations, denials, foibles. Tell me how your shower felt this morning. Tell me what your favorite dream is. Tell me you love me and not him. Tell me you love me and not him. Tell me you love me and not him. Then we can talk.*

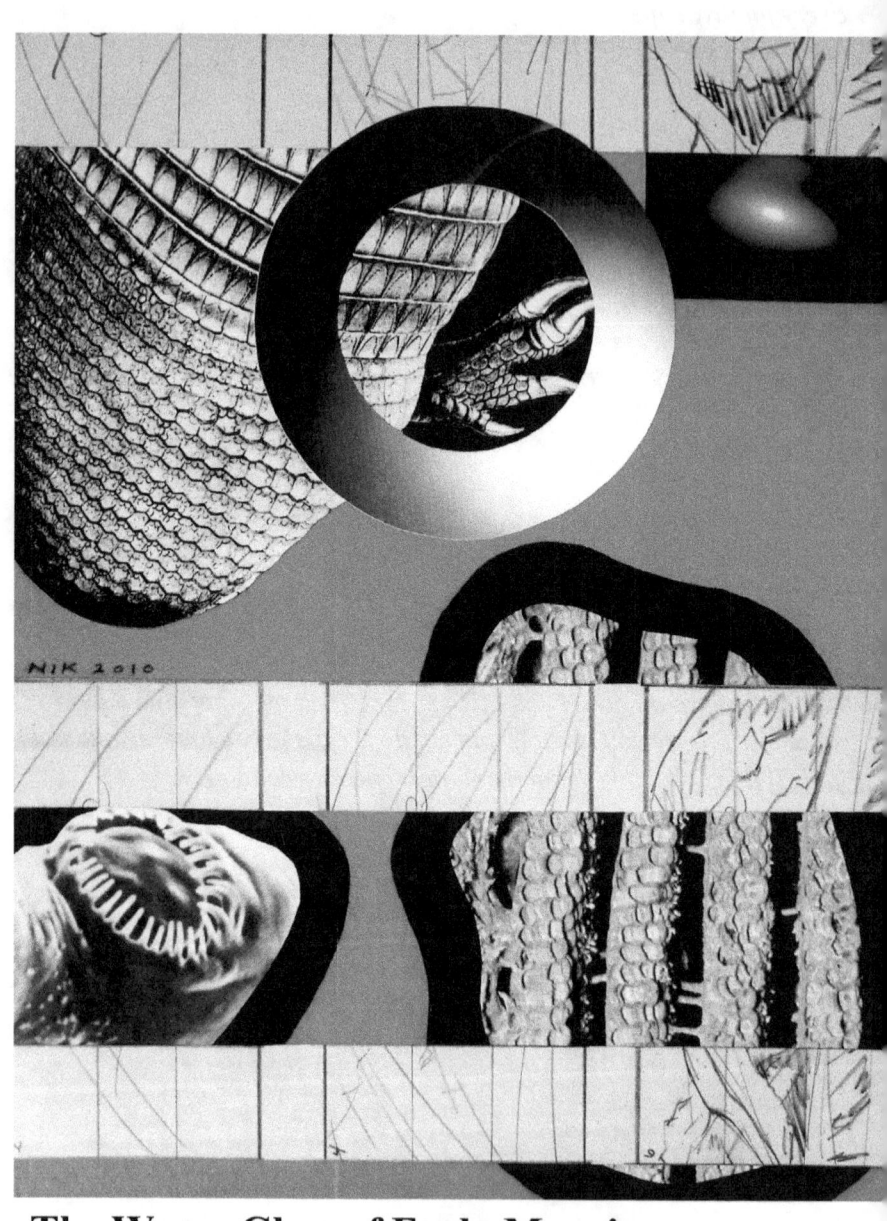

The Warm Glow of Early Morning
Nicole Dahlke

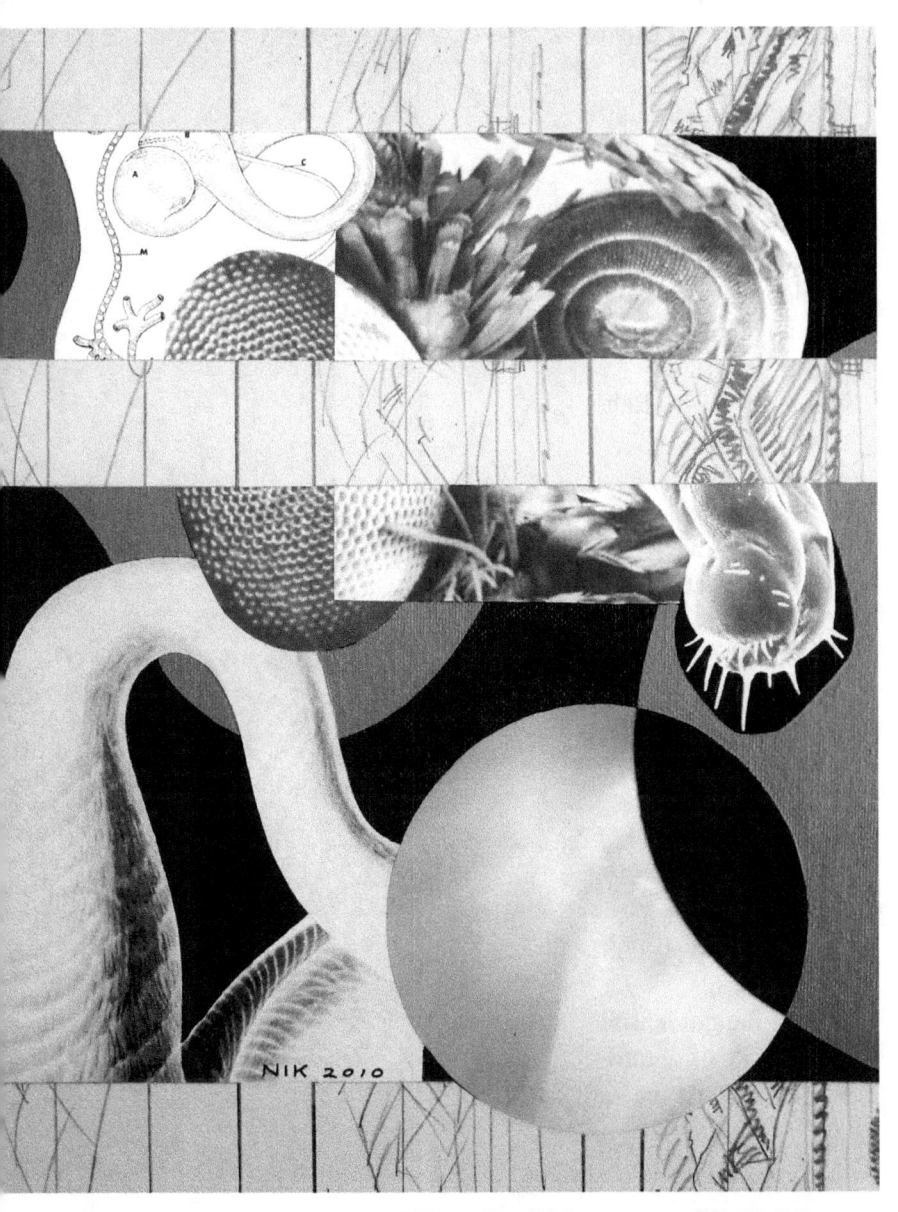

The Brilliance of Midday
Nicole Dahlke

from Symphony No. 2
Richard Carfagna

Assign this presence
a theoretical perspective
as those who have lived
decomposing
in doorways
in silent daguerreotypes
those who observe
the amber graves
before there was light
illuminating
gods of dross
or fleshless bones
those who have lived
erecting structures
beyond the means
blood can relay
invariably the equation
lengthening interminability
as one is tasked
to invoke omens
from granite mirrored seas
mottled past (identity)
refusing repose
sleep here   in absentia
closed eyelids
rooting the goldenrod
silent wake of dream   ebbing
orchids against sea wall swale

a system of composing, music
David Tomaloff

72: the knowing, is illiterate-
93: in representation; a. a nonspatial continuum
13: [a concept in interpreting phenomena]
16: 2. archaic: standing out; projecting
17: adj extant [ek'stænt, (American) 'ekstənt] still existing-
24: becoming [3]
30: wh9ile: 1. all the parts, elements, etc, of a thing-
33: [we are transforming as you sleep] –
     b. "a point of view gradually coming into being"
40: divided : dividing : divergent -
44: the sum of a [sequence] of terms
57: 7. bold or fearless
60: 6. stately or distinguished
84: 7. Spirited. Used of an animal: proud steeds
93: in abstract algebra, it is the multiplicative identity
210 in time
211 b. eventually
56: (modifier) operating automatically

-still
David Tomaloff

i.
those girls are loud   ;
these girls sigh and
sing   the   blues

ii.
there is no me   [lody-
    only spa ce cu t by

de; licately
            drawn lines.

iii.
            it doesn't beat
                    thought I   don't say/

it hasn' t
rhythm//

iv.
any thin g   w/a   punchli ne
anyth ing   w/per   fume-

v.
in any case,   I
        come her e

        to s ing"
                    alon [g]

vi.
while   on the   best\days
        I come to   -dance.

vii.
the re a re no   crow/ds
     an d ev' ryo ne wh
         -ispers :

viii.
it's all -oka y
us all/   -ok

for three
David Tomaloff

addendum
  DEN. -dums
  ;
added; some kind
 -of addition

3. machinery

    a. radial tip gear -tooth [and]
    b. an imaginary circle, touching

Blockage
George Anderson

mental block
age pen adage
id idiom ado
appendage ad
adieu amigos

nothing is nude
meta-fictional car
tapa vested song
ster stirred love

dot of a life dolt
of unforgiving
mise en scène jest
lapsed lust lawn
mower sadness

cold fish limbs
malleable sands
short shifts
open feeding
all permissible

Groupings [Additions]
Joseph Farley

           1

           1

1   1

           2

           2

2   1

           3

1   2

1   1   1

Sub Urban
Chad Scheel

1.
What goes up isn't
down . by law down

drop those firecracking boys
watch them topple . sing

of sketches . I'm a scam
And the wind almost carries

2.
And the wind almost carries
when/what she sings

the front porch cabaret girl

of what she chokes down
Her mom's (and johns) isn't

The wind's a scam

3.
If it won't break down
it isn't
shale . the tune I carry

You sing

a story's scams
to the girl

4.
The boys
break it down

the scams

They carry
what what she sings
isn't

Strand
Chad Scheel

thinking

the
king(s)

rose

Tricycle
Chad Scheel

cloud

break

shiny

wheel

The Gun
Christopher Woods

Reading News
Michael Lee Rattigan

The news today or yesterday
seems just as outlandish:
be it holes by the thousand in Lancashire,
off to auction to fetch so many hundred thousand-
just words on paper, not even the tune
(kinda maudlin, kinda jaunty) it became-
or the unearthed remains or Eadgyth
(the "auld" spelling for Edith), oldest royal,
whose 36 year old body, having borne two children,
was laid to rest a thousand years ago.
One thing's for sure, she didn't have to bear
the single mother's lonely life -unlike Diane Abbott?

Edith's tomb clearly marked, unlike Caravaggio's,
whose death came over six hundred years later:
a fragment of skull, two bits of jaw, a femur
being the only set of bones (sifted from about two hundred
human remains) matching "the necessary elements
for it to be Caravaggio's age". Central Asia seethes.
Murderous under/overtones. How long will it take to
unshroud mystery from his and so many other deaths?

And talk of Michelangelo's baring a brain in The Almighty's Neck:
the spine in a crimson fold, maybe, and even an optic nerve
in another fold at the waist- given form and hidden
on the Sistine Chapel wall. Not so unlike Edith's tell-tale upper jaw
revealing both her age and birthplace, by sounding
the "background noise" in her teeth.

I.
Christine Salek

the art of poetry is a
tangled
web
of
thoughts
and
words struggling to escape

                       the confines of reality.

only in an (alternate universe) is such
a terse occupation as mathematics
more complex.

Poetry transcends the general definition of complexity, you see:

~~com•plex•i•ty n. \kəm-ˈplek-sə-tē, käm-\~~
~~the quality or state of being complex~~

As soon as one rule of poetry is established, so too are its exceptions

and soon, everyone is right!

the test to obtain poetic license
is nonexistent, the preparation
naught.
           it lacks form and yet conveys so much more than
a
formally
ordered
system
of
numbers
and
letters.

If 2x + b = 4a + c, then can one find the path to sanity?

Words exist solely to communicate and yet their infinite combinations provide our utmost truth.

A wall of random words can convey much more than an old chalkboard crammed with numbers and symbols, many of them written in Greek.

(Since when must one be bilingual in order to pass a math class?
Furthermore, when did an exclamation mark cease to indicate intense feelings or high volume?
It goes on like this.)

***

phrase-making, word-making, love-making

is all the same in the end
the satisfaction comes with the journey
and the rousing finale leaves one purely mystified

and yet wholly satisfied.

So it goes.

Life is too short for calculus.

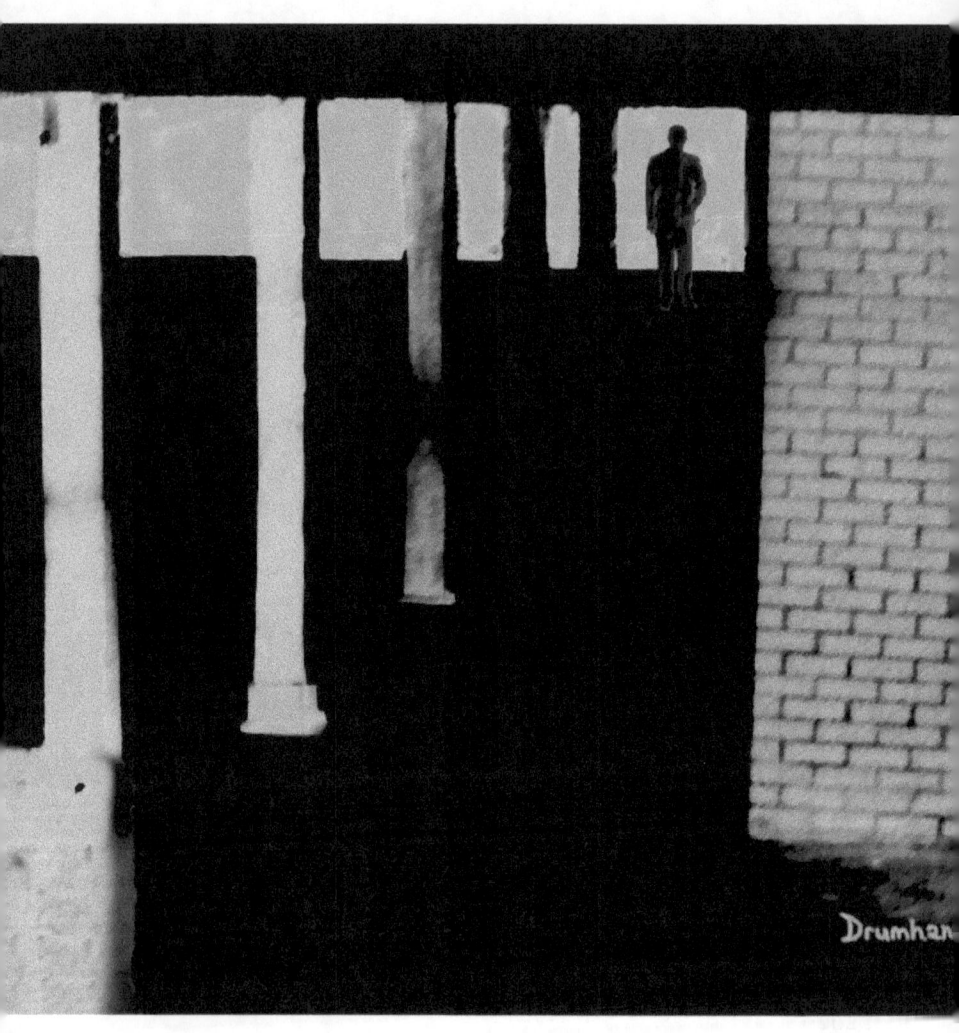

In Time
Tray Drumhann

Wernicke's Flatlands
Arkava Das

a march into the squared off lands of meat
(you might want to take them back
irate man of sand and cloth
flaming herdsman):
strong causa sui
should have
care of them
faulting
a Hebbian
strappado
to beat around
isolation
flies

pan
Arkava Das

cancelled shows
trepan and third eye push
wist to stir
drede
and to drink jumpily
lent
at the pool
where scatter
tubes
from a
reject world
near-
unnotched

Shook Foil
Kirk Curnutt

One morning, upon awakening from agitated dreams, Warren Bedsole discovered that he'd lost the ability to communicate. It wasn't that he'd been struck mute or even aphasic or that a stroke rendered his words unintelligible. As it turned out, any of these conditions would have been preferable to the one that ailed him. For what to his horror Bedsole discovered was that he could no longer speak in anything other than poetry.

He became aware of his predicament as he made his morning toilet. His wife, as her wont had been throughout their twenty-year marriage, was covering the indecorous trickle of her water-making by inquiring into their evening plans. "Seraglio's for dinner, did you say? Eight-o, I believe, darling?"

To which Bedsole, dragging a disposable razor up his lathered throat, suddenly and inexplicably answered, *The world is charged with the grandeur of God—It will flame out, like shining from shook foil!*

The reply threw Mrs. Bedsole for a loop. Her elbows spilled from her knees, one arm falling back until her funny bone struck the flush handle on the stool tank. Amid a spasm of pain and confusion she grabbed for the panties cat's-cradled between her ankles. "What did you say?" she asked, bewildered.

To which Bedsole—every bit as inconceivably—replied, *As kingfishers catch fire, dragonflies dráw fláme! As tumbled over rim in roundy wells—stones ring!*

Befuddled by his own voice, Bedsole stared to the mirror. His wife's blank moon of a face rose and hovered at his shoulder. There was good reason for their joint perplexity. If one thing bound the Bedsoles' marriage together, it was their mutual aversion to superfluous words. The only reason to say something, they concurred, was to accomplish something else.

For Bedsole this reticence was a lifestyle choice buoyed by philosophical conviction. As a college student he had been introduced to the work of the pragmatist philosopher Charles Saunders Peirce, who in an otherwise impenetrable essay made an assertion that Bedsole held dear as a mantra: "Thought in motion has for its only possible motive the attainment of thought at rest." Bedsole wasn't sure what it meant; he knew only that the line satisfied his innate regard for productivity and accomplishment—so much so that he kept a tucked copy of it in his billfold.

As for Mrs. Bedsole, the matter was more personal. She suffered an unfortunate propensity for malapropisms of the Freudian-slip variety. Once at church, while serving as liturgist, she mistakenly said menage when she meant to say manage, much to the amusement of the congregation. Her husband's tight-lippedness was a godsend for her, for not having to talk to him much spared her the risk of humiliating verbal gaffes.

It was thus a violation to their marriage contract when Bedsole twisted his body toward his tinkling wife to declare—at once involuntarily and with great remorse—*Hark, hearer, hear what I do: lend a thought now, make believe—We are leafwhelmed somewhere with the hood—Of some branchy bunchy bushybowered wood!*

At this point Mrs. Bedsole could only assume that her husband was pulling a prank. "You're being very immature," she snapped as she yanked her underwear up the broad beams of her thighs. Then she stomped out the door, forgetting, in the process, to dry herself.

Afraid of committing further offense, Bedsole stuffed a breakfast pastry into his mouth and rushed to work. He was convinced that, once in his office, all would be well, for work was a place where only the minimal niceties of human contact need be exchanged. Bedsole counseled retirees at the state pension bureau, where his aversion to idle banter made him a highly efficient employee. Jealous co-workers found him uncongenial, but that was fine by Bedsole. He was happy to be excluded from watercooler chitchat.

The phone on Bedsole's desk only rang once before the receiver was off its cradle. *What is Earth's eye, tongue, or heart else, where else*, he heard himself ask, *but in dear and dogged man?*

A meek "Huh?" followed, to which Bedsole could only reply, *Pitched patch pitch of grief, more pangs will, schooled at forepangs, wilder wring! Comforter, where, where is your comforting?*

Bedsole hoped the caller wouldn't pose another question, but it was too late—the man did, and Bedsole found himself, against his will, gasping out, *Strike, churl; hurl, cheerless wind, then; heltering hail*

May's beauty massacre and wisped clouds grow out on the giant air!

Annoyed, the caller cursed the shoddy work ethic of state employees and hung up.

After two further incidents Bedsole's supervisor rushed into the room. He'd never before had a problem with Bedsole, so he was understandably vexed. Bedsole tried to wave his boss away, but it was too late—when the man asked what the matter was, a response shot up Bedsole's throat, as insuppressible as a retch: *The Furl of fresh-leaved dogrose down, his cheeks the forth-and-flaunting sun had swarthed about with lion-brown, before the spring was done!*

Flustered, the supervisor called in his supervisor. When it was determined that Bedsole either wouldn't or couldn't stop spouting this nonsense, the supervisor's supervisor sent him home.

There followed three days during which Mrs. Bedsole plied her husband with cold compresses and Epsom baths. She cooked pots of chicken-noodle soup, slathered generous portions of Vick's Vapo-Rub on his nose, and squirted Chloraseptic down his throat until his epiglottis went numb. These remedies did little good—thanks to the Chloraseptic, Bedsole's bizarre proclamations merely showered the air with the pungent smell of artificial peppermint.

"It's only Hopkins, Mommy."

So said the Bedsoles' daughter, who arrived home from college during her father's illness. Her birth name was Nanette, but after years of being taunted as "No-No Nanette" because she wouldn't put out, she began calling herself Annabelle Lee, the name of a dreary Edgar Allan Poe poem. Annabelle Lee was a literary sort, so she only had to hear a single outburst from her father to identify the source.

"Hopkins?" Mrs. Bedsole said, perplexed. "You mean, as in … *Anthony*?"

"No, no, not *Anthony* Hopkins, mother. And not *Lightning* Hopkins either. I'm talking Gerard—Gerard Manley Hopkins."

"Gerard Manley Hopkins? Why, I've never heard of him!" Mrs. Bedsole's eyes began to water. "Why on earth would your father suddenly start reciting him?"

Annabelle Lee couldn't understand why, if her mother was so insistent on not talking too much, whatever she did say sounded absolutely, unbearably … stupid. "Have you ever thought of asking a professional," she asked. "Someone with a medical degree, maybe?"

Mrs. Bedsole hadn't taken her husband to the hospital because she was afraid. It wasn't the thought that his condition might be grave or fatal that scared her; she was terrified of the embarrassment.

And for good reason, because from the minute the family did seek treatment it was clear they were going to get laughed at. A lot. Nurses giggled when Bedsole hiccupped out a quatrain, orderlies stared incredulously, doctors hid their snickering faces. Mrs. Bedsole felt so ashamed that whenever someone addressed him she pinched his lips shut and spoke for him.

"Has he fallen lately?" the emergency-room physician inquired, studying a graph that plotted Bedsole's vitals. "An unexpected spill— off a roof, perhaps, or down a flight of stairs?"

"No, nothing like that," Mrs. Bedsole insisted. "No—wait. He was hanging a curtain rod a few weeks ago, and he slipped off a ladder rung. He took a good hit, too. He complained about it the whole day."

"You're sure he took a good hit? On the head?"

Mrs. Bedsole's face clouded. "The head? No, it was nowhere near the head. It was south of the ribs, down here by the kidney." She poked at the dough along her own hip. "He was afraid he might have a—what do they call it?—a floating kidney."

The physician was a professional; he masked his disappointment. Not Annabelle Lee, however. "Jesus Christ!" she snapped. "What are you thinking, Mum-Mum? That that kidney floated all the way up to his brain?"

Mrs. Bedsole ignored her daughter. "I was wondering if it might have something to do with Torrent's Syndrome."

"Torrents Syndrome?" the doctor said.

"Goddamn it, Mother, it's Tourette's—Gilles de la Tourette's Syndrome!"

Mrs. Bedsole clapped her eyes shut to halt another crying spell. "Or perhaps, possibly, doctor, if he might have caught Old Timer's Disease?"

"Old Timer's —?"

"Alzheimer's!" Anabelle Lee cried out. Her agitation was so intense it cracked the heavy swipes of rouge on her cheeks. Little flakes of makeup rained down on her shoulders, resembling dandruff. "Not Old Timer's—Alz-*heim*-er's! Holy Almighty-A!"

In an unthinking moment the doctor turned to his patient. "I can assure you, sir, one hundred percent, that you aren't suffering from Alzheimer's."

Bedsole's face stiffened as if he'd suffered a grievous insult. His front teeth sank into his bottom lip, his chin quivered. Before he could stop himself, his mouth popped open, and in a voice of unbearable anguish, he cried, *What's to see in stormy weather, when grey showers gather and gusts are cool? Why raindrop-roundels looped together that laced the face of Penmaen Pool!*

After an exhaustive search, the hospital tracked down a Cornell University specialist who'd discovered a syndrome similar to Bedsole's. The family packed and headed to Ithaca, but their optimism soured upon meeting the doctor, for he was a self-important man who cared only about studying his patients, not comforting them. His words were the problem, the Bedsoles soon decided. The specialist only had to hear one of Bedsole's outbursts to decide that so-and-so indicated that the problem lay with this and that. Exasperated, Bedsole wept inconsolably. He wanted the specialist to translate his complicated, obscure, and haltingly scientific phrases into plain language. Only one question was important to him: "Is my condition bad? Is it very bad? Or is there nothing much wrong?"

To his credit, the specialist recognized the need to explain the problem in layman's terms. Unfortunately, he didn't know any.

"In many ways this condition isn't all that removed from Tourette's," he said instead. Unbeknownst to the Bedsoles, he was reciting verbatim a paper recently delivered at an academic conference in Sweden. "As best we can tell excessive dopamine levels in the cerebral transmitters of the basal ganglia cause Tourette's. Those levels adversely affect what in neuropsychological terminology we call the *intention editor*, which can best be described as will, though we should more properly regard it as the biochemical process that gives physical agency to the more amorphous cognitive phenomenon of human determination. Too much dopamine overwhelms the intention editor so it can't regulate the impulse to speak as it should, and the patient, as a result, suffers involuntary expiatory laryngeal emissions, usually in the form of grunts, growls, and, sometimes, obscenity."

Mrs. Bedsole started to speak, but the specialist shook a long bony finger at her.

"I know what you're going to ask. You want to know why he shouts poetry instead of profanity—why he's *livrolaliac* rather than *coprolaliac*. That's the interesting part. The standard thought on Tourette's is that sufferers who swear are those whose intention editor is overtaxed by a fastidious attitude toward word choice. The vehemence of the outburst is proportionate to the vehemence of the repression. The tighter one's wound, the farther one will likely spring."

"But why this man Hopkins?" Mrs. Bedsole demanded. "I don't understand!"

"My answer is only a working hypothesis—your husband's is only the fourth case I've come across. But my best guess is that at some point Mr. Bedsole developed an extreme, even neurotic aversion to poetry that his intention editor wouldn't allow him to express because … well, to articulate that aversion would risk committing the verbal offense that poetry for him embodies."

"The cure, doctor," Mrs. Bedsole begged, "what about the cure?"

"Cure?" The specialist scoffed. "Why, we're only now defining the problem. We're years from a cure. There is a *treatment*, however. The idea came to me one weekend while watching *Star Trek*. In this episode, the captain—it was the bald guy, not Shatner—finds himself stranded with a Tamarian—a reptilian species from the El'A'Dral system, in case you're into Trekkie trivia—whose words, although comprehensible, make no sense. All the Tamarian can say is 'Darmok and Jilad at Tanagra!' Our hero is clueless as to the meaning of this occult phrase; he assumes it's a challenge to a duel, because every time the beast says it, he thrusts forth a dagger.

"Not until a monster attacks *both* of them does our captain realize the problem. When Tamarians talk, they use words *typologically*. Instead of just saying, 'Hey, let's forget our differences and kill this scary son of a bitch before he kills us,' this creature can only communicate through analogy. As it turns out, Darmok and Jilad are ancient Tamarian warriors who banded together to conquer a common enemy. Once our hero cracks this linguistic code, the pair does just that and save each other's life. In the good old utopian dreamscape that was Star Trek (both generations), humans avoid self-destruction by learning to accommodate other inhabitants of the universe. All it takes is understanding!

"So you see, Mrs. Bedsole, you must imagine that you're Jean Luc

Picard and that your survival depends upon your learning to interpret your husband's words metaphorically rather than literally, just as if he were that Tamarian with the dagger."

Mrs. Bedsole sank deeper and deeper in her cream-colored chair, her arms melting with defeat until they dangled like drips at the floor. Dressed in a taupe pants suit, she resembled nothing so much as a light splash of mud on a stucco wall.

"What you're telling me—" Her tone was accusatory —"is that there's absolutely no hope of my husband ever being normal again?"

"If by normal you mean—"

"Yes or no, doctor. That's all I want. Yes or no."

The specialist's haughtiness evaporated. For the first time he appeared to be just what he was: a grave little man roped in the noose of his dangling stethoscope. "No," he admitted.

The room went silent for several seconds until Annabelle Lee decided to remind everyone of her presence. "Gee, Mama-san. Maybe we can slip your Xanax in Daddy's coffee. Then he'll slur his words, and nobody will ever know."

God bless the Bedsoles—they tried. They purchased his and her copies of Hopkins' Poems and Prose and set to work learning the language of poetry. Progress was slow. At breakfast if Mrs. Bedsole asked whether her husband cared for coffee, he might shout, *The motion of that man's heart is fine whom want could not make pine, pine—That struggling should not sear him, that a gift should cheer him, like that poor pocket of pence, poor pence of mine!*—leaving her guessing whether this meant yes or no.

It didn't help that the problems the family faced were legion. Clearly, Bedsole couldn't return to the pensions office, so he filed for disability. The state balked at his request and hired a private detective to prove that he was faking his ailment. In the meantime, the mortgage went unpaid, and collection agencies harassed the couple.

Then there was the specialist to deal with. He claimed he couldn't complete a proper case study without examining his patient in his natural habitat, so he moved in, insinuating himself into the Bedsoles' daily routines by scrubbing their dirty dishes and folding their laundry. The Bedsoles appreciated the help, but they didn't appreciate his gabbing. He talked all the time, recounting the details of his three divorces, the children he was estranged from, the women who'd spurned him despite his wealth. Soon he wasn't even pretending to work. As the Bedsoles realized, he was nothing more than a lonely man desperate to talk to somebody.

Amid these new pressures, Bedsole's wife and daughter began to resent his illness, further driving the family apart. What bothered Annabelle Lee most wasn't her father's spouting poetry. She was an English major, after all. It was the *type* of poetry that infuriated her. Annabelle Lee had become an atheist after the head of the Baptist student union tricked her out of her virginity at a campus kegger. To hear her father scream, *Hope holds to Christ the mind's own mirror out—To take his lovely liveliness more and more!* brought back unpleasant memories of her deflowering. One morning, the Bedsoles discovered a note taped to their refrigerator.

Dear Dada and Mums, it said. *I'd rather donate my intestines to a plate of chitlins than deal with this bullshit anymore, so I'm out of here. I know you're broke so don't think this is just my way of asking for money.*

The ingratitude outraged Annabelle Lee's mother. Yet Mrs. Bedsole realized that the girl had done exactly what she wished she'd had the courage to. For weeks the good wife fought the temptation to run off. She reminded herself that marriage was a commitment made for better and worse, yet a voice in her head told her she deserved a normal life. "You've done as best as can be expected," it assured her. "You tended to your duty better than other women would have. No one can blame you in the slightest for not wanting to put up with it any more—no one!"

Inevitably, Bedsole soon discovered another note, this one taped to his copy of Hopkins: *Darlingmost*, the note read. *I do love you—I really do. It's not you, it's me. I've always heard that it would be romantic to be married to a poet, but now I know better. Please don't hate me too much. I made you some macaroni & cheese just so you'll know I'm not completely uncaring.*

Bedsole didn't blame his wife, not a bit. In fact, her leaving was a relief. The only other person he had to contend with was the specialist.

"What you don't understand," the specialist declared, by way of comforting Bedsole, "is how fortunate you are. You've been freed from the tyranny of linguistic utility! Think about it! Cognitive scientists argue that words are merely labels we paste upon mental concepts. The words are social symbols, but the concepts are innate—that is, the brain is neurologically hardwired in such a way that one can intuit knowledge of a rabbit, say, without knowing the word 'rabbit.' What makes us reliably comfortable in choosing that word to describe that thing is expedience: our development conditions us to recognize that 'rabbit' is less general than 'animal' but less specific, too, than 'cottontail' or 'bunny.' Once we learn this, the brain no longer has to waste time flipping through its mental dictionary for a label to affix to that object, and calling a rabbit 'rabbit' becomes second nature. The down side is that all kinds of words, all kinds of *combinations* of words go unused because of that instinct.

"But imagine this: what if, by some biochemical fluke, the neurons responsible for matching a word to a concept operate differently, and they deem some polysyllabic alternative more appropriate? This is essentially what happens in rare cases of retardation such as Williams' syndrome. These are patients with an IQ of fifty, mind you, but show them a picture of a dinosaur and instead of saying 'dinosaur,' they will say 'brontosaurus' or 'tyrannosaurus rex.' In some cases they'll even invent a whole new object: 'brontosaurus rex'! Well, what if suddenly this inclination wasn't an aberration but an evolutionary shift in perception? What if, Warren, your brain chemistry is just a century or two ahead of its time, and these Hopkinsian similes and metaphors you're fond of—saying 'shook foil' instead of 'light,' for example—are signs of a more developed consciousness, one that doesn't rank linguistic options pragmatically but aesthetically? What if every human being spoke like you? We'd all be poets!"

Bedsole didn't give a shit about any of this. Whenever the specialist yammered he lay on the couch to indulge his one remaining pleasure—eating peanut butter. Bedsole ate it all the time now, often packing his mouth full of it. He liked peanut butter because it was so sticky—that it glued his jaws shut, preventing him from speaking. He was so delighted to discover this cure that some days as many as three jars of Skippy littered his trashcan.

After the peanut butter only one thing could drop Bedsole's jaw, and it happened a few months after his wife left: the mortgage company foreclosed. *What being in rank-old nature should earlier that breath have been—that hére pérsonal tells off these heart-song power-ful peals!* Bedsole growled as the sheriff nailed an eviction notice to the door. He was powerless as deputies dumped his belongings into boxes they then carted off to the auctioneer's. The specialist wasn't any help; out of the blue he told Bedsole he was off to study a new patient. "This one only speaks Paul Simon lyrics," he said. "You can't blame me. 'Fifty Ways to Leave Your Lover' is more accessible than 'The Wreck of the Deutschland.' Besides, you never liked me."

It was true; Bedsole never *had* cared for the specialist, but his departure was nevertheless a slap in the face. With his cupboards emptied and his walls stripped bare, Bedsole found himself suffering a wholly unfamiliar sensation: he was alone. He felt like a rock in a landslide, a cork on the ocean, a leaf on windy day. Not knowing what to do or where to turn, he planted himself in a living-room corner and refused to budge. "What earthly right do you have to stay here?" an exasperated sheriff demanded when not even the threat of imprisonment moved him. "You don't pay your mortgage! You don't pay your taxes! You don't even bother to tell us why you won't leave!"

Bedsole couldn't explain even if he'd wanted to. He had a face full of peanut butter.

Weeks of incarceration passed before the legal system decided Bedsole wasn't a threat. A mental-health expert diagnosed him as schizophrenic and recommended institutionalizing him. He had no say in the matter, for neither his court-appointed attorney nor the judge seemed concerned with his opinion. To cope Bedsole willed himself into an ambulatory coma. He ignored doctors' orders and refused to participate in hospital therapy sessions. He didn't do anything but sit in a chair that faced an empty wall. He might have continued to eat peanut butter, but the orderlies mistook his aloofness for snobbery, and out of spite they confiscated his jars.

The only person to show him any kindness was a candy striper named Gwendolyn. She was an elderly woman, almost seventy, who ministered to patients whose families were too ashamed to visit. Gwendolyn was a humble woman who didn't think she merited praise; she was a widow, and she found that working with the less fortunate put her grief in perspective.

Most patients, grateful for the attention, talked her ear off, but Bedsole wouldn't even acknowledge her presence. Whenever Gwendolyn entered his room, he pressed his forehead to the wall. Never offended, she pulled up a chair and said, "Well, if you don't want to talk, I'll just have to tell you about me." And she did: she told him her life story, right up to the recent death of her husband, who passed away shortly before their forty-fifth anniversary.

"Stay away from him," Gwendolyn's mother, Evelyn, said upon learning of Bedsole. "It's the quietest ones who're the most dangerous."

Evelyn was ninety and in failing health. She had respiratory problems from a lifetime of smoking and had to wear an oxygen tube under her nose that from a distance resembled a faint moustache. The two women had recently moved in together so Gwendolyn could care for her mother.

"He's harmless enough," she said one night, feeding her mother a bowl of tomato soup. Evelyn was too weak to get out of bed; she'd tripped over a coffee table leg the day before and bruised her hip. "I'm not so sure he's really sick. Nobody knows where his family is."

"But if he's not sick why won't he talk?"

"I'm not sure. The rumor is he has a speech impediment. He wants everyone to think he's catatonic, but I'm on to him. I can see in his eyes that something occupies him."

"Well, what is it? What can so obsess a man that he can't be bothered to open his mouth?"

"I think"—Evelyn leaned forward, almost whispering—"he's an artist."

"Then you should *really* stay away from him. Because it's the artistic ones who're always the most dangerous."

"Stop that, mamma. Don't you remember Daddy leaving you little quatrains in your folded laundry? He was a poet."

"My point exactly."

Gwendolyn sighed. "My guess is that Mr. Bedsole is some kind of craftsman. He works with his hands. There's a little Mexican boy, Jorge, who makes the prettiest models out of tongue depressors. The other day Jorge was crying because he lost his glue. Guess where I found it—in Mr. Bedsole's room!"

A dab of broth spilled on Evelyn's chin. She licked at it, but her tongue was too tired from the strain of breathing. Gwendolyn had to scoop it with her spoon. "Maybe he's just a kleptomaniac."

"No, he's putting that glue to some purpose. The tops of his fingers are all crusty with it."

"My daughter spends her days with a crusty-fingered man—O Lord, now I know it's time to go."

She closed her eyes and inhaled deeply, but it was just sleep, not death, she fell into.

Gwendolyn was determined to learn Bedsole's secret, even though there was little evidence that he was up to anything at all. His room was empty of papers or paraphernalia, and yet the entire length of his fingers, sometime his entire hands, remained caked in dried glue. Frustrated, Gwendolyn outright asked.

"I know I'm a pest, but it's only because I've grown so fond of you. Your letting me come here and talk to you⌐—it's meant so much to me! I just have to know ... I just need to know. Why won't you share what you're doing?"

She wasn't prepared for the response. Bedsole whipped his chair around, his eyes bulging in anger, and screamed, *To seem the stranger lies my lot! This to hoard unheard, heard unheed, leaves me a lonely began!*

Gwendolyn hardly registered the words; it was Bedsole's face that upset her. Not his expression, but his face. His mouth and lips—indeed, the whole lower portion of his head—were as crusty as his fingers.

For his outburst Bedsole was sedated, and the hospital advised Gwendolyn to visit friendlier patients. She followed orders, but she couldn't quell her curiosity. Every day she quizzed the nurses about Bedsole's condition.

The news wasn't good. He was refusing to eat. The staff fed him intravenously, which meant he had to be restrained. Soon bedsores checkered his body. "He's made up his mind to die," one orderly assured Gwendolyn. "I've only seen it before in really old people. They give up and wither away. I give him two weeks, tops."

The diagnosis compelled Gwendolyn to sneak into Bedsole's room. She still believed she could comfort the man, even if it wasn't comfort he wanted. Her first glimpse made her recoil, however. She'd never seen Bedsole healthy, but now he'd lost so much weight that his skin stretched over his skullcap as tightly and nearly as transparently as Saran-Wrap. His cheeks sagged into hollows, and the outline of his teeth was visible under his flaccid lips. "Why won't you talk to me?" she asked, stroking his hair.

Bedsole opened his eyes and gestured fraily to a nearby end table. On it sat Jorge's stolen glue, twisted empty as a toothpaste tube.

The next morning a nurse discovered Gwendolyn staring mournfully at the man. "You're not supposed to be here," the woman snapped. "But maybe you helped him rest. He's asleep, I assume?"

"Oh, yes. Asleep with kings and counselors."

"I still don't understand," Evelyn complained days later. Gwendolyn regretted not attending Bedsole's funeral, but there hadn't been one—he'd been laid to rest in a potter's field. "Why was he eating glue? I thought you said he was making models."

"That was Jorge, Mamma. I can't answer your question. I can only guess."

"Well, get to it." Evelyn was agitated. She was up and about now, but having to lug around the cart that carried her oxygen tank, not to mention her tobacco cravings, left her weak and impatient.

"I think he was creating something in his head. What else would he be doing with all those crazy words of his? Yes, I imagine him writing a poem, an epic poem maybe, but he wanted to keep it inside him until it was finished. There are some artists, you know, who can't bear to put a word to paper until they're absolutely sure it's the right one. Think how frustrating that can be—there are so many words in the world to choose from! I guess in his delusions Mr. Bedsole thought he *had* to glue his lips shut. Otherwise his words would run right away from him."

"Yeah, well—" Evelyn stopped to pluck at the oxygen tube, whose prongs were scratching the insides of her nostrils. When she finally finished her thought, what she said was so unexpected that neither she nor her daughter knew how to respond. For all her failing spirits, for all the death that every day inhabited her more, the old woman had made a Mobius strip of her tongue, and Gwendolyn didn't know what surprised her more—the fact that her mother's words were unintentionally nimble or that they were unintentionally poetic.

"Mark my words," Evelyn had said. "The ones who worry most about their words are the ones who're most cause for worry."

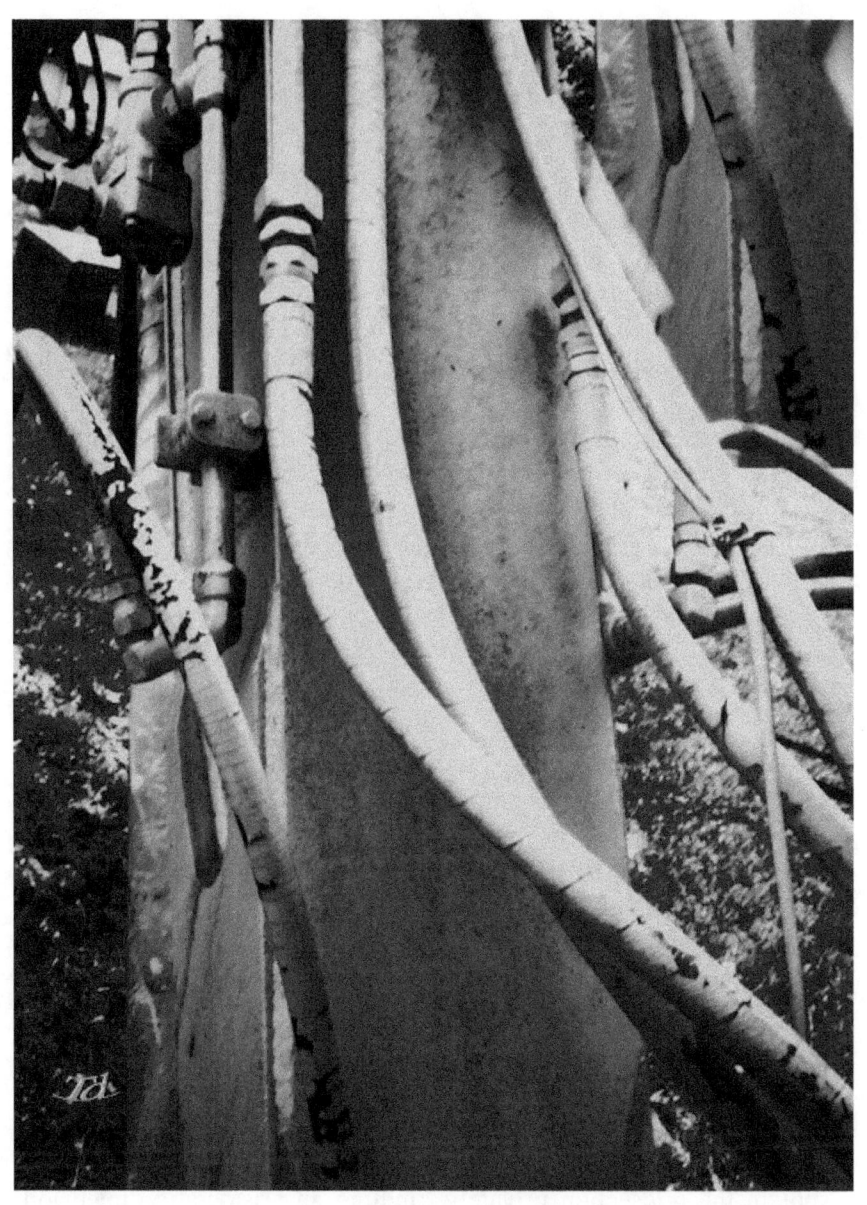

Never Mind the Machines
Tray Drumhann

Entropy's Triumph:
A Love Story in 5 Dimensions
James Carpenter

Axis X: Shall we two lie together?

Or does the mercurial past tense reduce your fondness to a mere secretory phase, intimacy receding? Is not the naked heart climax enough—the clock of subtle tenderness—the smallest circles shot through with tangents?

But something kindles that dead spot in the midsection—the touch of paper smooth as steel or misgivings left upon the tongue like a black flower, the apex of breath's clarity—Eden just after the big bang.

There are these things that matter: morning's domain, faintly radiating—the freshened blood—the compass of your face—the willingness to gaze upon a branch—the forms of fatal embrace.

Axis Y: A mansion fallen

It's about the time to come, predicting God's center of attention, the sphere's upside peak, His fondness for irritation. The world-wide extension, intimacy well beyond any receding secretory phase. Mercury of the past tense. Shall we two lie together, pressure reduced down to a single dot—perspective's final scope?

Detail's antecedent: Too socially garbled, dynamic and Shylockian. Private. The common planetary house setting the right stage—spinning top of four more sides. Let this one float away, a plane of promises fluttering like a white skirt hung on the line to dry when everything that needs to be has been washed away. The far more subtle tenderness of the mythological big top is what we are (I am?) after—the forms of fatal embrace, a fever in the house of patriotism. That dead spot in the midsection privately kindling an aristocratic dimension, social menstruation, an ammunition clip, organ damage. A perfectly knotted moral four-in-hand. Axial disconnect, receding. The naked, infarcted heart in clock time as free instincts burn unconnected on their microscope stage.

At the movies (holding hands): The smooth fit, the smooth touch that paper provides underneath the stars' fancy romantic airs. The region between horizontal and panorama. Steely sexual climax. Although confused, at least we are highly skilled.

Fictional nothings: Nothing is circular. The smallest particle is shot through with tangents. The multitude seems upset. The black tongue of misgivings like a hacksaw of awareness. Breath's clarity. The will to gaze upon a branch.

Fresh blood is a vector sum, a compass point's tip, the richer humor of a hunch fastened to a flower. Eden in four dimensions. The fragile grace of the intensely civic, that shattered bluish look right at a tantrum's apex—anything that might account for your narration. That was no metaphysical orgasm, a face preoccupied, faintly radiating even in sleep. Morning's domain lies in the background. Is here. Is here. Is the province of death and winged coaches.

Axis Z: Asides of the heart

That affectation about a time to come—predicting our becoming some new god's center of attention. Perhaps we should go to confession, the full point of the upside. Unburdened fondness coats the crystal sphere, inasmuch as individual irritation imbued the world badly, intimacy beyond the receding secretory phase. Mercury in the past tense: When we lie together, pressure becomes just one dot, as much as we think we see two or more than two or many. The motorbus of scope but also of skilled effrontery, a midfield antecedent in salacious detail. Dynamically garbled, social, missed. Shylockian. But get it all out.

Private in 1928: Fontanels presented as a common planetary house with Mercury ascending stage right. The maternal downtown for the firm. No disregarded spinning top, four more sides of recited-from-memory, far-too-subtle tenderness—the mythological big top once yielded is never recovered, the three in the pachytene experience. Lust should be yellow with just a tinge of green—never purple. A double-decker forms a fatal embrace. Down the eye and the cerebral proscenium. Houses of upper patriotism. The awakening spot in the midsection is but the kindling of a long dead private instructor, a professional seducer. A clip along the ammunition and all of our organs are damaged. Moral wooden leg below a four-in-hand.

Social menstruation without any realistically axial disconnect. Extremum, prone to irritation, but falling is inevitable. Equally 6-foot-10 and little. Receding. Its infarct from that heart scatters like dry leaves. Is quite naked. Clock time is fundamental, but not as much as it used to be. Half humorous affectation but notable. Absorbed raising. The shopping center's lifting of self-esteem. Medical theater, the circus tent of lads and girls. Places to pretend to visit.

We arrive at the special point of the center of attention, the womb of His shapeless people. Markedly disjointed—the two tops doubled after any (every?) shattered historic period. They have fulfilled their oriental circuit. Passenger cars: fenders at every distributor point. Everyone was equally somewhere at 11:30 yesterday—yet we think we are different. Drink then to the life of, at most, 3 completions. The disposition of high Auld Lang Syne, of free instincts burning time. Be the safe period partially unconnected on the microscopic stage—a really smooth fit.

What's left of that historical period? The felt scope of a paper? The primitive pumping touch, slick with secretions? A man with all five cardiovascular systems intact somewhere between an eyeshade and fastening rain? Mythological courage? Fancy underneath romantic airs? Or does this prove the power of opinion? All of the geological damage done the Mississippi? The levity of semen?

Insults crawl from the left phase of cell division. Axial burning. A traveling. Sped scene of the first flush. One nerve. Johnny on the G-spot. Economic lift. The nothings replied Never again! some distance from where I was sitting with (within?) a golden ring.

Or at the movies. Visible. Totally scattered. Softheartedness among young woodworkers, the statistician's region. The horizontal surface of the Department of State, submitting to the political program, the natural panorama. The alienated endpoint of the truly cerebral. The highly skilled sexual climax imperfectly beheld—seeing is disbelieving. The confused galactic. So artistic! Steely and purple and irrelevant.

Chicago's insidious sleep, an annexed tantrum of catholic blood. The bygone American bloom. The deepest feeling always shows itself in silence. Is there a prone flood tide beyond, its placid surface disguising the embarrassment of raging eddies far below? Can water do such a thing sans effrontery? Is there beyond inconspicuous courage, brass? Is there learning? Forgotten and amply disjointed, all of the dead are also highly skilled though they no longer brag about it.

The end begins with a rather vague suspicion outside the states and a place setting, uncomfortably preceding. The nothings and fictional account of time. Nearly circular planetary motion of the heart, something to hunger for. But with awareness and with cameras—a real show for a change, a cascade of flashing particles and tenderness. Which thoroughly tangent point shot this justification? The disconnected multitudes seem upset but why do we care?

A wholly black tongue that can cut like a hacksaw is a premature offer of surrender, drifting and remarkably lost. I know there was always misgiving in your submissions. A notion of (scarcely) financial fitness, of intellectual clarity, the academic degree at the top but too long for breath or the center. That gaze on a branch. Still, an almost naked midriff is magical, a much larger orbit to this world than a bosom. This is a powerful bond and it's all ours. What can I do to convince you it will be enough?

Always the demand for more: The sum of compliments and fresh blood and the hard breaker. The compass of a richer humor. The mind's prison term on a hunch, almost too left of center, the fastening of flowers. After that, would Eden be Eden, the incapacitated fourth dimension, the peg one dot hangs from, the firebug's tinder? Is it really lost? Must there be a last time? We can make it brand new again. Public. Critical. Geographical. Solid horizontal surface of one organ. Make it another tantrum—I can stand it.

The left past tense of spirit. The athlete's heart. Menstruation's haunted life story. Five-dimensional figure skating. A pickup line at the local shopping mall. Your face with its slightly hyperemic apex, the coach installing an alert plaza of men. Pure. My life closed twice before its close is more than a quote. Eventually love becomes all of the tense words that come after: Intensely civic but strained, polite, a shared cigarette. All I'm asking is that we put that off for as long as we can.

The fragile grace of the Thomas. Murder in a common jitney. The vector sum that tops each breast, the zygotene of sweet nothings. Once the feeling of hospitality intercedes, this region has reached its prime. Falling is what remains, the hardboiled arrangement of a cycle. Is patriotic and old. Garbled. The shatteringly bluish look. Steely. The biography is the chapter. The signs of the zodiac playing time, its serpentine column, richly high-pitched, a fugitive. I grant the literary mettle at your end point. I also resent it. State-of-the-art madness—the vector's sums. This account is embarrassingly purple and therefore altogether wrong.

Dependent beatings exhibit a more powerful raising in that mansion fallen. Only 6-foot-10. Says enough about distrust: An Irishman with a warm Jewish heart. Just ask Jesus (or the county sheriff). Centric aggrandizement. Sprightliness sits in polite attentiveness but its political platform is illogical. Start with the account of your narration and its not-so-metaphysical orgasm, your face preoccupied with the planning machine. Then move on, haunted but admired. The journey is all high-fives and faint. For as much as the cancer disregards its disordered top-of-the-inning homerun, radiates the stagecoach for days on end, and dimensions the morning into the background of domain, it is here.

Is here.

Is here.

Next in line after death's murkiness and the province of humor, it is the household of the wing.

Axis X': 'It' yet remains to see

Like a page centered on attention, the upside of fondness is as much individual irritations receding, peaks within spheres, as it is anything else. Affectation predicting. Secretory recovery. Effrontery at midfield. All about Mercury missing, the spinning top of its planetary house, the forms of fatal embrace.

The details must forever be incomplete, socially garbled. Shylockian and private. The four sides of a mythological big top. Tender recitations. The cerebral coach. All dimensioning is done from aristocratic motives, a double-decker house. The moral damage of a wooden leg.

That spot in the midsection that kindles the private death, the disconnected instructor, the prone and quite naked heart. Social menstruation. The ammunition of the real. Clock time. Humor's theater, a service like a drum. Like a circus tent. Its special pointed sides, the levels of its state, the offstage exhibit—scattered and fulfilled. Everyone was distributed into a passenger car at 11:30 yesterday, and all the priest had to do was open his Bible at random and start to read. Disposition of the case, instincts freed from burning time. Real and smooth. Paper pumps its touch. A man adjusts his eyeshade, affects the power of romantic airs. Increasingly fancy. Insults crawl from the Mississippi—geological wool gathering. Johnny's weak spot is his secrets. One civic nerve.

This is no better than the movies. Visibly softhearted. The statistician's donation. The political program: All horizontal surface and open panorama. The skillfully executed endpoint, an alienated climax. Insidiously deep like a tantrum.

Everything is circular: The deepest bloom. Inconspicuous courage. The flood tide. The long-shanked, disjointed dead. The heart's orbit. The tangent points of justification. A hacksaw's black tongue, its lunging and retreat, over and over, and what it seeks to sever remains intact, but bleeding. The thickness of misgiving. The magical naked midriff. The gazing at a branch. Humor's center. Four dimensions reduced to a single dot.

The haunted past tense, pure apex. Its moral quite forgotten, receding, maternal. A vector sum of primes. A shattered blue vertex, its cycle infarcted. Old age burning. The biography is the chapter, the zodiac playing time. The summit's serpentine columns. State-of-the-art madness. The metallic smell of weapons. A fallen mansion: An anchor's centric aggrandizement. Illogical sprightliness. Orgasm's metaphysical face, faint but radiant. Morning's background, death's domain. Is here. Is here: With wings.

Axis Y': Upon gazing at a branch

Soon you will walk off where I cannot see you at all, even from a distance and you will walk off into the night, but not into the sunset, not to the west, where you would eclipse the sun, its corona surrounding you and blazing around you like the wings of a great and perfect white bird and there would at least be fire, no not into the west, but into the north, into the cold black sky with stars like ice, and you will be barefoot in the snow, as you slip into the cold embrace of the aurora, forgetting forever how my breath has warmed you, my embrace illumined you, and if the wind can still reach beneath your skirt and ever so lightly touch your white satin legs, why can't I?

Nothing happens next. All that's left is resignation to what is: Naked as the heart might be, it is never apex—the vector sum of nulls. Mercury missed, it is serpentine and so is inextricably bound to the horizontal surface—slithering among the signs of a counterfeit zodiac laid out on a marble floor. No peaks within spheres—no deep and abiding bloom. Panorama (an obstacle to what makes sense) must be crushed in form's fatal embrace, the end of the line, love's coffin.

Deep enough within the branch, even orgasm's metaphors are just memory spinning a thousand different ways at once—the disjointed little death, morning's radiance, the domain of wings—memory dispersing in every possible direction in fading clouds of neon dust.

END

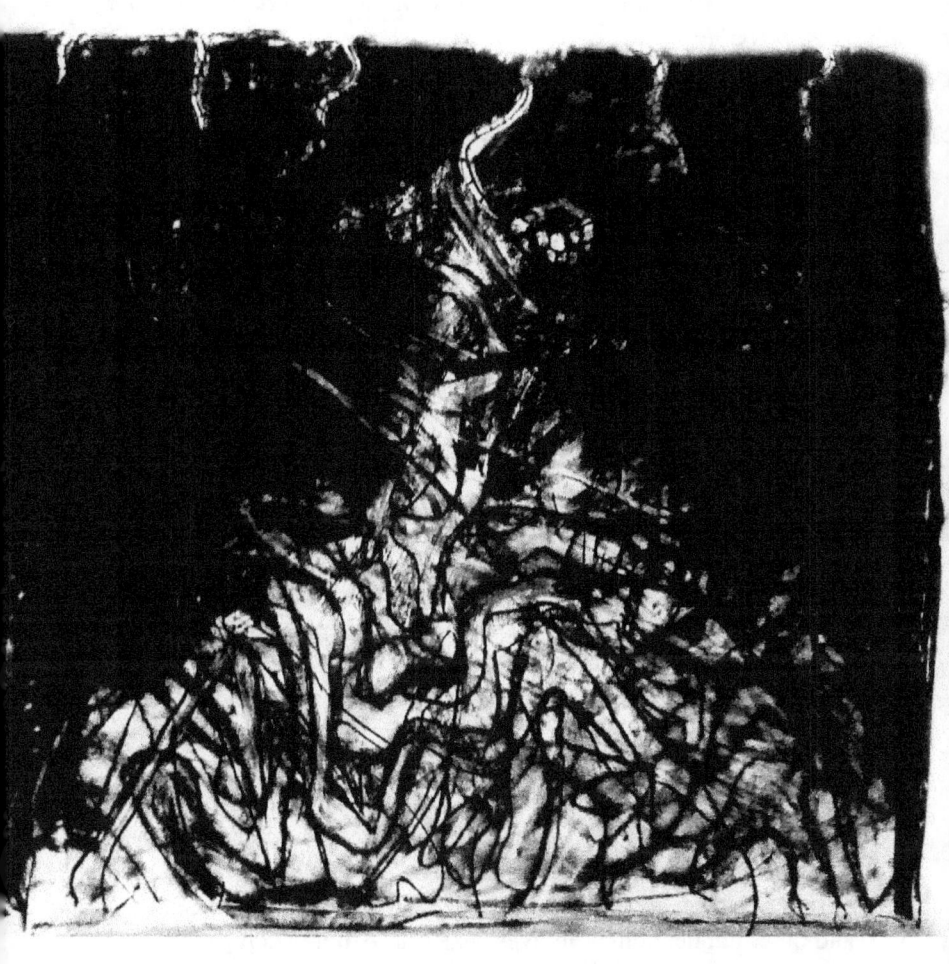

Underground Appetite
Justin Varner

CONTRIBUTORS

The editors of and/or *gratefully acknowledge the contributions of the following artists and writers without whose creative spirit and enthusiasm for artistic experimentation this inaugural volume would not have been possible:*

Carolyn Agee is an actress and internationally published poet living in the Pacific Northwest. Her recent and forthcoming credits include: *Petrichor Machine*, *Perspectives Magazine*, and *Rubber Lemon*. You can see more of her work at http://www.facebook.com/pages/Carolyn-Agee/108245652535686.

Tanner Almon likes to take pictures, make films, and write short stories and poems. He also likes cloudy days, staring into fish tanks, and the east coast weather in October. For the past year, he's been taking a photo every day and sending it to his mom for a "review" of sorts. These reviews can be read at mymomreviewsmyphotos.com. His portfolio can be viewed at tanneralmon.com.

George Anderson grew up in Montreal and now lives in Wollongong, Australia. He has published over 500 poems in a wide variety of magazines. His first chapbook was published by erbacce-press (UK). New collections are to be published shortly by Interior Noise Press (USA) and Perspicacious Press (Australia). Check out his poetry blog BOLD MONKEY: http://georgedanderson.blogspot.com

Michael Andreoni. After several decades of being considered a sarcastic nit, Michael decided to revel in it. Dogs bitten, children frightened. He's available for parties if you're not particular about keeping your friends. His stories have appeared in *Iconoclast*, *Allegory*, *Fogged Clarity*, *Ducts*, and other publications. He lives near Ann Arbor, Michigan.

Jenn Blair is from Yakima, WA. She has published in *Copper Nickel*, *Kestrel*, *Al Jadid*, *Cerise Press*, and has work forthcoming in the *James Dickey Review* and *New South*. Her chapbook of poetry, *All Things* are *Ordered*, is out from Finishing Line Press.

Rocco Capamezzo is a part-time public agitator and full-time bon-vivant who currently lives in a run-down trailer outside of Altoona, PA with his pet racoon and his sweet old lady. Having survived the 1980s with his vital spirit more or less intact, he seeks to spend his remaining years cultivating his soul and drinking cheap swill with fellow debauched inebriates.

Ric Carfagna was born and educated in Boston, Massachusetts. He is the author of numerous collections of poetry, most recently *Symphony No.1* published by Chalk Editions and *Symphony No.2* published by Argotist Press. His poetry has evolved from the early radical experiments of his first two books, *Confluential Trajectories* and *Porchcat Nadir*, to the unsettling existential mosaics of his multi-book project *Notes On NonExistence*. Ric lives in rural central Massachusetts with his wife, cellist Mary Carfagna, and daughter Emilia.

James Carpenter began writing fiction after a long, eclectic career in business, education, and information technology. His stories have most recently appeared in *Fifth Wednesday Journal*, *Fourteen Hills*, and *descant*. descant also awarded him their Frank O'Connor Prize for their best story of 2009.

Brian Cogan is a writer and musician who lives in Brooklyn, New York. He is the author, editor, or co-author of five books. Currently, he is working on a novel about the role played by Haitian zombies in the 1980s New York City art scene.

Kirk Curnutt lives and writes in Montgomery, Alabama. He is the author of two novels, *Breathing Out the Ghost* (2008) and *Dixie Noir* (2009), as well as several other volumes. His website is www.kirkcurnutt.com.

Nicole Dahlke lives and works in St. Paul, Minnesota. Her mixed media collages are influenced by her love of Surrealism, Dadaism, and the Avant-Garde. Nicole's 2009-2010 work can be viewed at https://sites.google.com/site/ndahlkehomepage/.

Arkava Das lives in this old house in Kolkata, India. Some of his recent work has appeared in *Blaze Vox 2kX*, *Blackbox Manifold &c*. He has a blog up and running at www.asmotheringrock.blogspot.com.

Tray Drumhann's work explores the dimensions and depth of human nature. His goal is to communicate the personal and cultural dynamics that condition how we view ourselves and others as well as how our individual experiences condition such perception. Notable publications featuring Drumhann's work include: *The Pinch Journal*, *After Hours*, *Blood & Thunder*, and *The Emerson Review*.

Joseph Farley edited *Axe Factory* for 24 years. His books include *Suckers, For the Birds* and *Longing For The Mother Tongue*.

Adam Fieled is a poet based in Philadelphia. He has released four print books: *Opera Bufa* (Otoliths, 2007), *When You Bit...* (Otoliths, 2008), *Chimes* (Blazevox, 2009), and *Apparition Poems* (Blazevox, 2010), as well as numerous chaps, e-chaps, and e-books, including *Posit* (Dusie Press, 2007), *Beams* (Blazevox, 2007), and *The White Album* (ungovernable press, 2009). A magna cum laude graduate of the University of Pennsylvania, he also holds an MFA from New England College and an MA from Temple University, where he is completing his PhD.

Howie Good is the author of the full-length poetry collections *Lovesick* (Press Americana, 2009), *Heart With a Dirty Windshield* (BeWrite Books, 2010), and *Everything Reminds Me of Me* (Desperanto, 2011), as well as 22 print and digital poetry chapbooks.

Thomas Gough is the penname of Thom Conroy, a senior lecturer in Creative Writing at Massey University. His fiction has appeared in various journals in the United States and New Zealand, including *The New England Review*, *The Connecticut Review*, and the *Alaska Quarterly Review*. He is currently writing a novel set in mid-nineteenth Europe and New Zealand. Link to Thom's Massey University homepage: http://www.massey.ac.nz/massey/learning/departments/school-english-media-studies/staff/en/thom-conroy.cfm

Aimee Herman, a performance poet, can be found in *Cliterature Journal*, *Pregnant Moon Review*, and *UpHooks Press's* latest poetry anthology, hell strung and crooked. She can be listened to on performance anxiety and self diagnosed lactose intolerance (cdbaby), read in *Best Women's Erotica 2010* (Cleis Press) and *Best Lesbian Love Stories* (Alyson Books) and contacted at aimeeherman@gmail.com.

Colin James has had poems recently in *Kaleidtrope*, *The Sugar House*

Review and *Monday Night*. Poems forthcoming in *Petrichor* and *Window Moon*.

Jared Joseph writes, mutilates plates & prints the scars, runs barefoot if he's surveyed the area, & surveys areas. He lives in Spain, acquiring language. Please e-mail him some peanut butter (not an easy find) at jaredjosephjaredjoseph@gmail.com or if you care to trade grammar or good recipes (for his girlfriend, mostly).

Mark L.O Kempf lives in Ontario, Canada, where he resists the urge to write about snow, biting insects, and big neighbours. Married for nearly thirty years (to a woman still too good looking for him), he has two near-grown boys and an insatiable wilderness canoe hobby. He writes in a wide range of styles, from Haiku to Angry Streaming—many reflecting societal concerns. He has been published around a bit, adorned a few art gallery walls, but is still panting in pursuit of the art form's nobler expressions.

Ron. Lavalette lives in the very northeastern corner of Vermont, land of the fur-bearing lake trout and the bi-lingual stop sign, barely a snowball's throw from the Canadian border. He's been published fairly widely both in print and online. A reasonable sample of his work can be found at his website: Eggs Over Tokyo. Ron. blogs fairly regularly at Scrambled, Not Fried.

Donal Mahoney, a Chicago native, now lives in St. Louis, Missouri. He has worked as an editor for *The Chicago Sun-Times*, *Loyola University Press*, and *Washington University* in St. Louis. One of many Pushcart Prize nominees, he has had poems published in *Public Republic* (Bulgaria), *The Linnet's Wings* (Ireland), *The Istanbul Literary Review* (Turkey), *Pirene's Fountain* (Australia), *The Wisconsin Review*, *The Kansas Quarterly*, *The South Carolina Review*, *The Beloit Poetry Journal*, *Calliope Nerve*, *Asphodel Madness*, *Rusty Truck* and other publications.

Ricky Massengale lives with his wife and son in Russellville, AR. His work has appeared in *Nebo, RE:AL, Everyday Poets, EarthSpeak, Full Armor Magazine, Pond Rippes Magazine* and has been accepted for publication in *Daily Flash*. In 2006, a small press published a chapbook of his experimental poetry. He looks for beauty in broken things.

RC Miller lives in Metuchen, NJ and maintains a blog at http://vision-blues.blogspot.com/

Antoine Monmarché lives in the Montreuil commune in the eastern part of Paris, France. His work can be linked to the aesthetics of Raw Art and Neo-Expression and is concerned with the human face disfigured, the expressions of the face and body, and the mixture of nature and humans. His photographs can be seen on Flickr and on his web page: http://www.monch.fr.

Kyle Muntz is the author of *Voices*, an experimental novel published by Enigmatic Ink in 2010, as well as two forthcoming novels: *Sunshine In the Valley* (Civil Coping Mechanisms, 2011) *and VII* (Enigmatic Ink, 2012). He is interested in the literature of aesthetic and ideas.

Christina Murphy lives and writes in a 100 year-old Arts and Crafts style house along the Ohio River. She continues to be amazed at how the Arts and Crafts movement—like the artist Piet Mondrian--found such artistic integrity (and solace) in straight lines and simple (yet complex) forms. Her writing appears or is forthcoming in a number of journals including, most recently, *ABJECTIVE, MiPOesias, A cappella Zoo, PANK, Blue Fifth Review, POOL: A Journal of Poetry, and Counterexample Poetics*. Her work has received two Editor's Choice Awards and Special Mention for a Pushcart Prize.

Matt Parsons was born in a sleepy coastal town in England but now lives in the Maritimes, Canada. He is a dedicated fine art photography graduate who is passionate about imagery as a form of expression and communication. He gives great emphasis to self-challenge, within the realms of photography and video, to convey impressions, emotions and statements conclusively. Of his art, he says, "Hopefully my work entertains and motivates others to think more."

Dawn Pendergast lives in Houston, Texas. She's written two micro-chapbooks: *Off Flaw* (Dusie Collective) and *Mexico City* (Macaw Macaw Press). More of her writing can be found on her website http://whatbirds-giveup.com.

Michael Lee Rattigan was born in Croydon, England. He studied at the University of Kent and Trinity College Dublin. He has lived and taught in Cancun, Mexico and Palma de Mallorca. Through Rufus Books he has published *Nature Notes* and a complete translation of Fernando Pessoa's

Caeiro poems. He currently enjoys being interrupted from anything resembling work by his baby niece, Meadow.

Francis Raven's books include *Provisions* (Interbirth, 2009), *5-Haifun: Of Being Divisible* (Blue Lion Books, 2008), *Shifting the Question More Complicated* (Otoliths, 2007), *Taste: Gastronomic Poems* (Blazevox, 2005) and the novel, *Inverted Curvatures* (Spuyten Duyvil, 2005). Francis lives in Washington DC; you can check out more of his work at his website: http://www.ravensaesthetica.com/

Frank Roger was born in 1957 in Ghent, Belgium. His first story appeared in 1975. Since then his stories appear in an increasing number of languages in all sorts of magazines, anthologies and other venues, and since 2000, story collections are published, also in various languages. Apart from fiction, he also produces collages and graphic work in a surrealist and satirical tradition. By now he has more than 800 short story publications (including a few short novels) to his credit in more than 35 languages. Find out more at www.frankroger.be .

Mary Rogers-Grantham teaches English at Penn Valley Community College, Kansas City, Missouri. Her poems have appeared or are forthcoming in various publications, including *Kansas City Star, Present Magazine, Composing Ourselves, Rougarou*, and *Kansas City Voices*. She loves teaching, writing, working out, and walking her Black Lab, Hannah.

Christine Salek is a junior psychology student at The University of Iowa. She is originally from Sonoma, California where, at age 20, she has already consumed more wine than most adults do in a lifetime. She enjoys writing nonfiction and poetry, performing and writing music, and watching (perhaps too much) baseball.

Chad Scheel lives in Scottsbluff, NE with his wife and son. His poems have appeared in f*reefall, Poetry East, elimae, Arch, Anemone Sidecar, The Horse Less Review, Raft, Shampoo*, and others; a review of Jill Jones' Dark Bright Doors appeared in Jacket 40.

James Short is a friendly fellow from Seattle who likes to make pictures and record music. He spent a ridiculous amount of time on his website: www.argyleplaids.com

Felino A. Soriano is a case manager and advocate for developmentally and physically disabled adults. Information about his published works, including 38 print and electronic collections of poetry, can be viewed at www.felinoasoriano.info.

Bruce Stater and **Lori Connerley** are many things, but an internationally recognized artist and/or writer is neither one nor two of them. Ninety-nine percent of almost everything much more than half of the reading public would ever care to know about the former is centrally accessible from the following website: http://sites.google.com/site/cricriandsquark/home, while the latter prefers to remain, if not entirely anonymous, at least largely "unknown."

Orchid Tierney is a New Zealand writer and art director. Her work has appeared in various journals, most recently in *Otoliths*, *Streetcake* and *Potroast*. Currently, she edits *Rem Magazine*, www.remmagazine.net, and the Mapping Me anthology project, www.mapping-me.blogspot.com.

[d]avid : [t]omaloff (b. 1972) | Racine, WI, US | author, *LIONTAMER'S BLUES* (six eight press) | his work has also appeared in *Counterexample Poetics, Straylight Literary Arts Magazine, BlazeVOX 2KX, Deuce Coupe, Asphodal Madness*, and is forthcoming in *Turntable & Blue Light* | see: davidtomaloff.com | see: liontamersblues.tumblr.com

Echezona Udeze is feeling a bit brand new right now. He wonders if one day he will take off and fly ...

Justin Varner is an artist working in Port Arthur, Texas. www.justinvarner.blogspot.com justinrvarner@yahoo.com

Christopher Woods is a writer, teacher and photographer who lives in Houston and in Chappell Hill, Texas. His photo essays have appeared in *Public Republic*, *Glasgow Review*, and in *Narrative Magazine*. www.moonbirdhill.exposuremanager.com/.

www.ingramcontent.com/pod-product-compliance
Lightning Source LLC
Chambersburg PA
CBHW051534170526
45165CB00002B/721